Out of the Box!

Brand Experiences between Pop-Up and Flagship

gestalten

SURFACE TENSION

Page 6

725. 21 OUT

All That Matters

Page 70

Straightforward

GOING PUBLIC

Glamor & Drama

This is not a store; it's a story.

Once upon a time, there was a retail landscape. It was a flatland of logos and print ads, a two-dimensional terrain that one day began to morph into a three-dimensional brandscape and this is where the new commerce began.

With the ascendency of shopping apps, checking in and group buying, crowd sourcing and augmented reality, online shopping (e-commerce) and shopping from mobile devices (m-commerce), consumers can now research products, find the deepest discounts, get fashion advice from friends who are far from the fitting room, and have a say in how a manufacturer's next sofa will look or if it will even be produced. We can accomplish all of this at our keyboards, moreover, whether we're in our three-piece suits or our birthday suits. On the one hand, then, it has become increasingly difficult to peel us out of our pajamas and get us into the store. On the other hand, the internet cannot provide us with the kind of experience that moves us.

Walking into a shop today, we know the product specs by heart, but we don't know how its upholstery feels, how the shape conforms to our form, or if it will remind us of building forts with our grandmother's couch cushions in days long past. **A tectonic shift in technology and values is forcing brands to retrofit their approach to retail, event, and exhibition design.** More than a conventional showroom, today's increasingly apathetic customers need do-tiques, "fitting rooms" in which to try on both product and brand, places where the experience is as limited edition as the merchandise, and where brand, buyer, and goods are bound togeth-er in a catalytic chain—whether a financial transaction takes place immediately or later on.

Welcome to experience design. We solved the problem of displaying clothes on racks long ago, but learning how to seduce sensory-deprived and information-overloaded shoppers with a compelling spatial story is, well, a different story. Selling is about branding is about experience is about emotion. And emotion sells. The finest retail interiors, exhibition concepts, flagship stores and themed stores, temporary pop-up shops, gallery/boutique hybrids, and event spaces, mobile or sedentary, are becoming a form of media. Which objects, stores, and brands we choose will depend on which "channels" move us most. The shopper is a complex creature, with a fraught relationship to things, self, and style, with diverse interests, secret disappointments, and guarded aspirations. **Brands are learning that they must tap the visceral, intuitive, and imaginative core of the customer** and engage in a dialog with their "guests," who will spend time (or elect not to) in the universe created by the company. With galloping advances in technology, every shopping trip is poised to become a resented physical commute if the destination is workaday. Experience and the degrees of emotion that it engenders will turn a passerby into a customer, a customer into a repeat customer and a repeat customer into a Tweeting, Facebooking, checked-in advocate of the brand.

To make his week-long pop-up shop in Manhattan, fashion designer Richard Chai—who believes that the attention span of today's consumer lasts about two seconds—collaborated with Brooklyn studio Snarkitecture to transform the inside of a disused shipping container. The designers carved into blocks of EPS foam with custom-built wire cutters until a glacial brandscape filled the box, a monolithic white field, excavated, striated, with no truly vertical walls and no really right angles. Chai wanted to tap the senses, from the look of the interior to its sound and smell, to provide, as he phrased it, "an experience of exploration, an emotional experience."

As the demand for evocative, interactive, curated, and unrepeatable branding space continues to grow, temporary commercial interiors have anticipated experience design and brandscaping, and so deserve particular attention.

The pop-up shop began as a frills-free environment intended to relieve the high costs of brick-and-mortar retail—from long-term leases to interior design and architecture fees. It used to be that the only way to distinguish a pop-up shop from a back-room sample sale was the price on the hangtags, but in order to increase traffic and give pop-ups the aura of limited-edition destinations, the form grew increasingly baroque.

When British sports retailer Reebok, a pop paladin of the 1980s, opened a quickie sneaker store amidst the visual din of Manhattan's wholesale lighting district, local creative agency Formavision

frescoed every surface, including seating and displays, with nacreous honeycombs, chevrons, stripes, and polygons of every description. Borrowing from WWI dazzle warship camouflage and a 20th-century arts movement called vorticism, the storefront looked as two-dimensional and colorful as a comic book or a Technicolor version of Norwegian band a-ha's rotoscoped 1985 Take "On Me music" video. (Arguably a pop culture watershed that became the impetus behind the retail success of the leather motorcycle jacket following the video's MTV release.)

Artist Tobias Rehberger did a high-profile series of cafés in this vein. The temporary boutiques and brand sanctuaries of architect and former fashion designer Rafael de Cárdenas also share this audacious graphical approach, with robust contrasts of color and developments of form. For de Cárdenas, if these types of spaces are any good, they tell us two things: what is happening now and what will be happening soon, coveted information that the host brand must know and, through

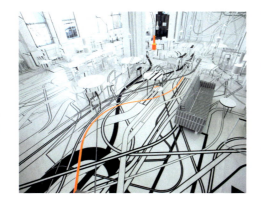

its spaces, broadcast. The projects on the following pages represent only a scant number of retailers and designers, but they exemplify the way in which codified rituals of product display are being superseded by bolder experiments (visually, materially, locationally, scenographically) to stimulate, as de Cárdenas calls it,

"never-been-seen-beforeness".

People just can't get enough of the new. And we don't just want to watch it, passively, on a screen; we want to step into it, climb it, row over it, slide down it, wear it, inhale it, get a little lost inside.

For the sake of expediency, the projects are divided according to their creative approach: graphic, material, straight, public/outdoor, and scenographic. As is shown in the first chapter, **Surface Tension**, spaces can be flattened or given dimension, become quiet or loquacious through the use (or avoidance) of color, pattern, typography, illustration, texture, or all of the above. They are caffeine or codeine, a graffiti-ed street and a gallery, articulations of progressive brands that want to be associated with art, culture, and innovation. In the following chapter, **All That Matters**, it is the material that says something about the label and, occasionally, delivers a message. **Straightforward** spaces give customers the relief of an unembellished, what-you-see-is-what-you-get experience and are commissioned by companies that value authenticity, candor, and a no-nonsense ethos while still putting a premium on good looks. The installations in **Going Public** locate the brandscape in a landscape, bringing the shop into the countryside or the countryside into the shop. Highbrow or low, high-tech or low-tech, material-driven projects are constructed from, for example, women's hosiery, industrial rolls of aluminium sheet, blue polyurethane foam, or rip-ties. Finally, **Glamor & Drama** presents brand stages in the form of novelty boutiques and scenographic interiors that appeal to our emotions in an effort to transcend the transaction. In the very best cases, customers buy into the business with more than just their money and consume, not just things, but culture, not just artifice but a sense of self. The purchase (if one is even made right away) becomes a souvenir of the customer's affinity with, not just loyalty to, the brand. So, as shopping pervades every arena of our public—once noncommercial—lives and wriggles into the machinery with which we fabricate our own identities, the most deeply experiential spaces could just become the poetics of the 21st century.

SURFACE TENSION

Graphics can both define and exquisitely confuse space. The mechanism behind graphical interiors is sometimes simple: Hundreds of stickers in the shape of black chevrons suggested abstracted flocks of blackbirds on the wing, making **ZMIK**'s boutique at the Basel art fair feel dynamic. Letters, in various point sizes and typefaces, gave texture to the **E-Types**' font shop in Copenhagen. Repetition, exaggeration, or layering can lend surfaces dimension, personality, mood, or depth. Taken to an extreme, this means that graphical interiors may feel deliciously disorienting: bigger or smaller inside than they appeared from without, or a profusion of contrasting color, geometry, or form. **Denis Košutić** slathered one of his Italian Amicis stores with such a variety of floral wallcoverings that the space could trigger a bout of hayfever.

At the pinnacle of the graphic aesthetic are several interiors, including the **Reebok Flash** pop-up shop in New York and a series of cafés by artist **Tobias Rehberger** that sprang from the trompe-l'oeil dazzle painting that once camouflaged World War I British Royal Navy battle ships. In a departure from his older dazzle projects, Rehberger didn't add any color to the bold line drawings with which he filigreed tables, chairs, and even window panes in the **Logomo Café** in Turku, Finland, but the illustration felt just as engrossing. In Flash, **Formavision** tattooed every surface with flashy geometries, garment racks appeared two-dimensional from certain angles, and furnishings—graphical devices just as much as the graphics—tapered to a needle point.

Somewhere between the bare and the baroque, however, there is a middle ground. **Tomás Alonso**'s trio of **Camper** shoe shops, for instance, feature a minimalist graphic look: Careful compositions of ceramic tiles make it appear as if some of them protrude from the wall when they are actually flush.

At their best, graphical interiors wake us up. They can connect viewers to something (the brand) far bigger than they are, or make a space feel intimate and the company that commissioned it, sheltering.

Kid's Republic
2005 / Beijing, China

SKSK ARCHITECTS:
KEIICHIRO SAKO
Client: Poplar Publishing Co., Ltd.
See also pages 26 and 122

The 165-square-meter Beijing location of Poplar Publishing's kids' bookstore is marked by a Candyland-like ribbon of carpet that cheerfully paves the interiors with "flagstones," so to speak, in seven colors. Zones in the ground floor event room—for storytelling, shows, and performances—are connected by 12 colored rings with various perimeters. Open spaces between sections of ribbon unfurling over the floor, walls, and ceiling are used for illumination or display. In one area, pale ribbons are staggered and layered to wrap an intimate interior and to create benches and a stage for a tiny auditorium. The ribbon itself as it climbs and descends serves as shelving, tabletops, gates, checkout counters, and seating. Apertures in the bookshelves become windows, passages, or cozy reading nooks so that children can sit or lie anywhere they like to read and play. The 100-meter ribbon meanders through the event space and up the stairs to the bookstore on the second floor, at one point turning into the steps themselves. If, traditionally, interior design restricts itself to narrow definitions of floor, wall, ceiling, and furniture, SKSK's design eschews these sensible and orderly definitions, suggesting instead that no distinction should exist between reading and playing.

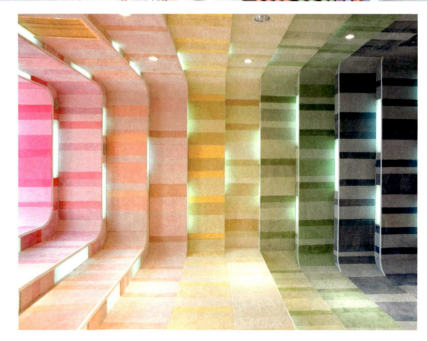

Unknown Union
2011 / Cape Town, South Africa

ARCHITECTURE AT LARGE: RAFAEL DE CÁRDENAS

Client: Unknown Union - Jason Storey, Sean Shuter
See also pages 44, 46, 48, and 52

The interior of Cape Town men's boutique, Unknown Union is another Pop Art-Op Art combo by New York-based Rafael de Cárdenas of Architecture at Large. In an 18th-century building,

two floors of retail space glow diffusely with ziggurats of multi-colored shelving, display cubes painted in vibrant ombrés of teal, green, lemon yellow, and pink, and an exploded chandelier of fluorescent tubes. Boxed in terracotta tile flooring (common in Cape Town) and white walls, the scheme was inspired by the simple forms and saturated colors used by Mexican architect Luis Barragán. A former Calvin Klein fashion designer, de Cárdenas tends to think of form separately from material. In this store—aptly since it sells clothing—he selected materials and surface treatments after settling on the forms, in much the same way that fabrics are matched to already determined styles in the design of garments

12

Brunner Fair Booth at Salone Internazionale del Mobile

2011 / Milan, Italy

IPPOLITO FLEITZ GROUP – IDENTITY ARCHITECTS

Client: Brunner GmbH

"All the stand's a stage...," one might say of the Brunner exhibition booth at the Milan Furniture Fair where the product was not simply a passive item on display, but the protagonist of a well-scripted installation. Brunner presented Twin, a featherweight, low-cost, monobloc plastic chair in a stage-like setting in an effort to appeal to architects as a "disseminating force" for the new piece. IFG designed the booth pegged to the slogan See/ Reflect/Act, cladding surfaces with artificial turf and melamine resin flooring and panelling walls with mirrored polystyrene shingles that were awash with several dozen chairs suspended in a maelstrom overhead. Mounted over the scale-like shingles, each section of the seating "storm" was rotated through 45 degrees, enabling visitors to view the chair from every angle in a gorgeously deconstructed explosion of color and reflections. The wall shingles also referred to the company's traditional, craft-based Black Forest origins and visitors could take away some shingles, printed with product information, as a souvenir of their visit.

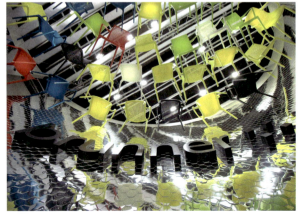

UNIQLO:

[1] Heattech Project 2009: 3 Global City Installations
2009 / New York, Paris, London

[2] Heattech Project 2010: Branded Art Installation
2010 / New York, USA

[3] XXL Space Invader Origami Santas
2010 / New York, USA

MONA KIM PROJECTS
Client: Uniqlo

For two years in a row, Japanese fashion label UNIQLO commissioned three-city, one-month branded Heattech art to re-launch an existing product line in its New York, Paris, and London flagships. Avoiding the usual retail tropes, Mona Kim designed bespoke, aluminium-framed monitors made of 100 Traxon LEDs that loop through synchronized video content and motion graphics to link product and brand. The next year, in New York, to convey the sensation of heat while contrasting high-tech with "no tech," a series of two to four-meter-high Sintra PVC foamboard fins appeared to change according to the shopper's point of view. To celebrate the winter holidays, the designer heat-folded Sintra again to create a four-meter-high hybrid of Santa and a Space Invader, both slightly "kowaii" (scary) and "kawaii" (cute).

[1]

[3]

[2]

Bond-In Diversity
2011 / Milan, Italy

KAZUHIKO TOMITA
Client: Dyloan Studio Milano

For a two-day, 280-square-meter exhibition celebrating fashion that ranges
from high-touch to high-tech at the
Milan trade fair grounds, Tomita used
Noah's Ark as a metaphor for a planet
in crisis due to our species' omnivorous
and insatiable consumerism. Garments
were displayed on flat hangers in the
silhouettes of endangered animals and
were hung from the ceiling to convey
a feeling of the lightness and tenuous-
ness of existence. The hull of the Ark
and a cresting wall of Sea Water share
the same surfaces, their abstracted
visual elements printed on ultra-fine
fabric stretched over a tubular structure, filtering air and light and shiver-
ing in the eddies of air created by
visitors moving through the space.
The exhibition subsequently traveled
for one week to a 350-square-meter gallery in the Leonardo Da Vinci National
Museum of Science & Technology.

Fitting Forward

2009, 2010 /
Hamburg, Germany

BITTEN STETTER, JUTTA SÜDBECK
Client: Fitting Forward

Fitting Forward is a Hamburg concept store designed by Jutta Südbeck and Bitten Stetter (author of the textiles book *Fitting Tales*) which has a different theme for its art, fashion, products, and accessories every two months. Stetter and Südbeck distorted perspective with the use of colorful graphics on top of deep black lacquered surfaces that de-emphasized corners and angles while a room-in-room-installation by the artist Arne Klaskala resembled a three-dimensional walk-in sketchbook. The first theme entitled *Talentiert—der Zoo der Einzigartigkeiten (Naturally Gift-ed—Zoo of Uniqueness)* was replaced by *Grosstadt Neurotik & Metropolen Massaker (Urban Neurosis & Metropolitan Massacre).*

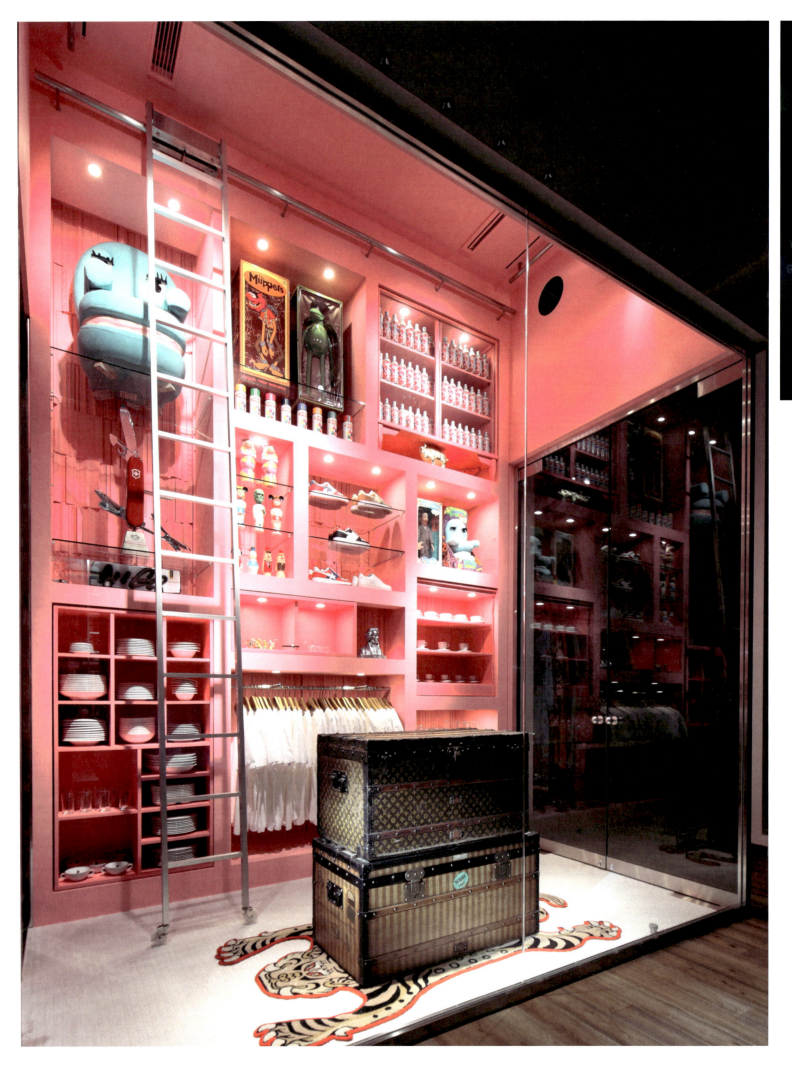

Pass the Baton
Omotesdando
2010 / Tokyo, Japan

WONDERWALL INC.
Client: Pass the Baton
See also page 128

Wonderwall's interior design for the Omotesando (and second Tokyo) location of Pass the Baton expressed the brand's appreciation of legacy objects and the value of passing down belongings that you love to the people you love, a value that also gave the brand its name. The museum- and library-like displays showcase the metaphorical flow of things through inheritance while a white box gallery suggests the preciousness of beloved objects.

[1]

Camper Shop
[1] *2011 / London, UK*
[2] *2011 / Glasgow, UK*
[3] *2010 / Genoa, Italy*

TOMÁS ALONSO
Client: Camper

For his first interior project, Galician-born, London-based Slow Design adherent, Tomás Alonso fitted Genoa's first Camper Together shoe shop with ceramic, bent steel and optical illusion, using simple but powerful gestures. For his second act, he did the same to create London's fifth Camper location in Covent Garden, which was followed by a third in Glasgow. The store's bespoke furnishings are the result of his ongoing investigations into hybrids of material and form (mixing the natural and synthetic, as in this case, lacquered tubing and white oak) and his signature method for bending steel tube. Alonso, a Royal College of Art graduate and OKAY Studio collective member, clad the walls in a grid of black-grouted though conventional white 10 x 10 cm square tiles. To these he added three irregular tile shapes in several colors, a combination with which he was able to generate multiple geometric patterns in isometric perspective. Tiled shoe displays protrude from the walls beside flat colored tiles that seem to cast their own shadows in paler shades of the same hues.

[2]

[3]

Eifini Chengdu
2009 / Chengdu, China

**SAKO ARCHITECTS:
KEIICHIRO SAKO,
KEN-ICHI KURIMOTO,
LIANG JU**
Client: Eifini
See also pages 8 and 122

The 160-square meter Eifini boutique ("floating" in Chinese) in Chengdu is part of a 180-location franchise that sells women's clothes throughout China. To emphasize the fashion, the Sako architects painted floor, wall, and ceiling white, allowing all architectural components of the space to recede. Furnishings, like the cash counter, were dressed in the same tiles as the floor, as if they had simply grown out of the floor. The only accent in the space, aside from the clothing, is a 250-meter-long violet hanger pipe, suspended from a clear acrylic pole, that winds freely through the shop, serving, variously as garment racks, curtain rods for fitting room drapery, an entryway, a mirror frame and the base of display tables.

Nothing Happens for a Reason at Logomo Café
2011 / Turku, Finland

TOBIAS REHBERGER
Client: Turku 2011 Foundation

As with the artist's other café interiors in Venice, Baden Baden, and elsewhere, Rehberger's design for the Logomo Café in Turku, Finland was based on dazzle painting, a technique used by the British Royal Navy during WWI to camouflage the speed, vector, and size of battleships. Except for the ceiling, Rehberger tattooed every surface of the space, running his pattern over Artek tables and chairs, and even window panes, making the white room and furnishings the canvas for an artwork drawn in black and safety orange (a departure from the previous projects and dazzle ships in that it is otherwise devoid of color). The linework was UV-curable inkjet printed and sealed into a PVC floor covering and wallpaper. For the artist, it was crucial that the work be made in a space whose function was not to show or be art, so that it comes as a surprise to the viewer on entering.

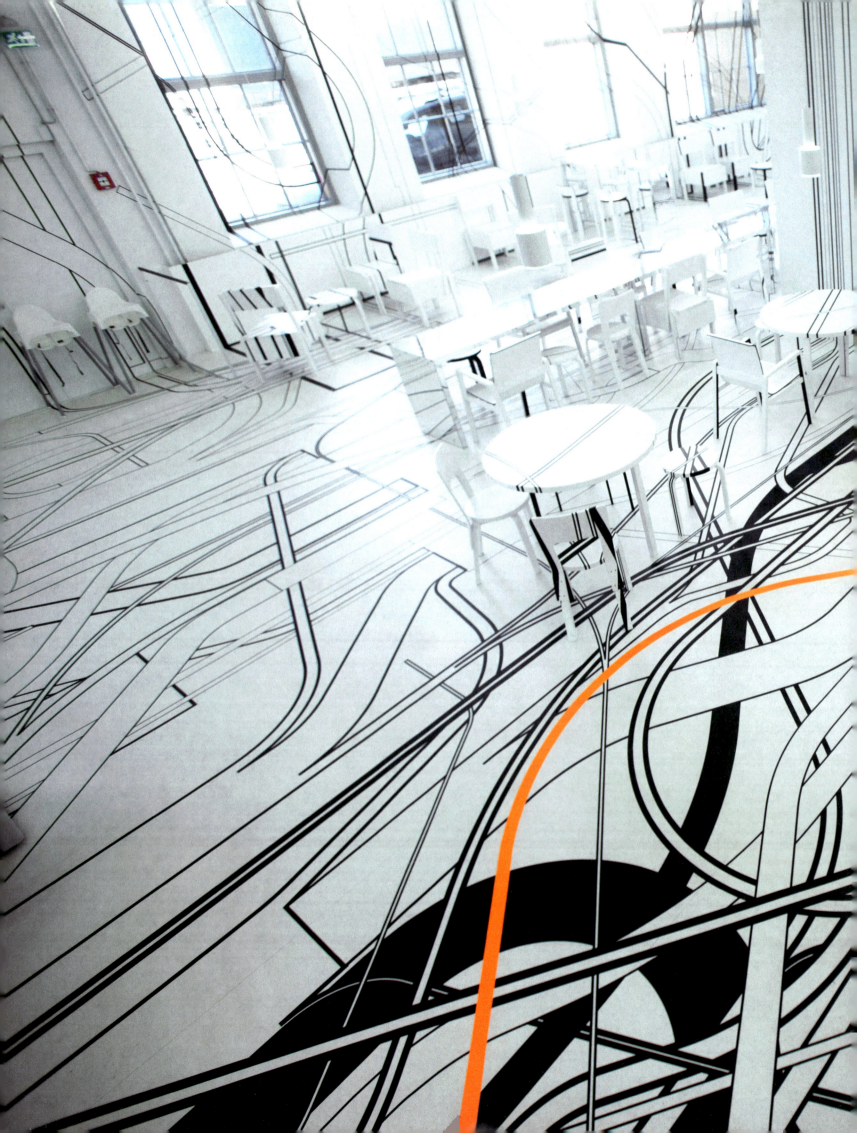

Artshop 09
2009 / Basel, Switzerland

ZMIK
Client: Sevensisters & Handmade
See also page 81

During the Art 40 Basel fair in Switzerland, ZMIK applied hundreds of self-adhesive black chevrons of varying sizes over the walls, floor, and ceiling of a disused cloakroom to create a temporary 120-square-meter design and art boutique run by Sevensisters. The stickers resembled a flock of birds migrating toward the shop and swarming thickly around a close-packed display. As the swarm grew denser, the chevrons appeared to change into a herringbone pattern.

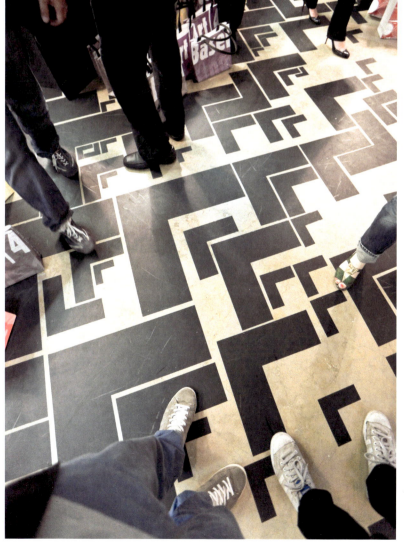

Kizuki + Lim
2010 / Singapore

TERUHIRO YANAGIHARA
Client: Less Is More Co. Ltd.

In central Singapore's Raffles Hotel, the latest installment in a series of hair salons for booming Japanese franchise Less is More injects modernity into a larger historical setting, reflecting the spirit of the company's young stylists. A glacier-like structure divides the interior into reception, cutting and shampooing areas. Large, pivoting, mirrored wings fold out of the cutting room wall; when closed, they rest flush with the wall, allowing the salon to become an events and performance space. The timbered reception "hut," features a small gallery space that also serves as a stage for performers.

Audi Q7 Coastline Marina Exhibition Stand
2008 / Miami, USA

MUTABOR DESIGN
Client: Audi
See also page 240

At the high-profile crossover art-design event, Art Basel/Design Miami, Mutabor associated the Audi Q7 Coastline performance car with adventure, in general, and with yachting, in particular. Their exhibition booth-cum-lounge-cum-boat deck framed the car in faceted forms and oversized objects in marine styles, but rendered in timber decking. Thinking of it as an "elegant yacht on wheels," they used aluminum elements and planking inscribed by hand by the Dutch typographer and "letter man" Job Wouters, aka Letman, with the names of visitors to the booth. Letman's elaborate white calligraphy alludes to the boat building industry's lush craftsmanship.

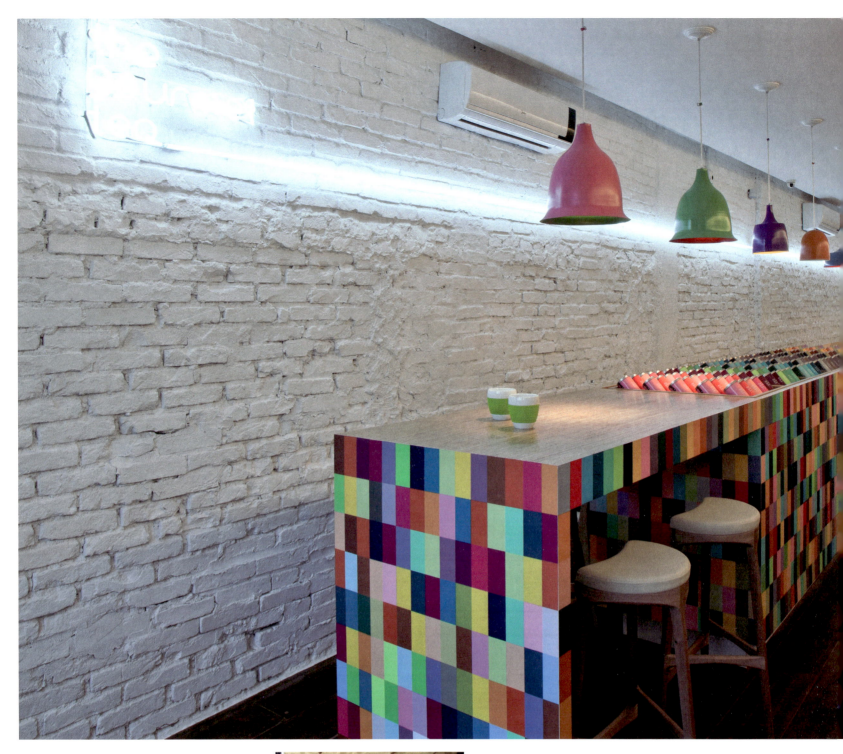

The Gourmet Tea
2011 / São Paulo

ALAN CHU
Client: The Gourmet Tea

Plywood furniture dressed up in multi-colored adhesive tape serves to organize the brand's first Gourmet Tea Lounge + Store in São Paulo. Inspired by the colored tins of the company's 35 tea blends, local architect Alan Chu provided a minimalist, economic solution. After exposing the structure and extant bricks, Chu painted them white; he preserved the original floor, lowered the ceiling in order to eliminate the distraction of existing beams, and arranged indirect, continuous lighting to emphasize the depth of the long, narrow building.

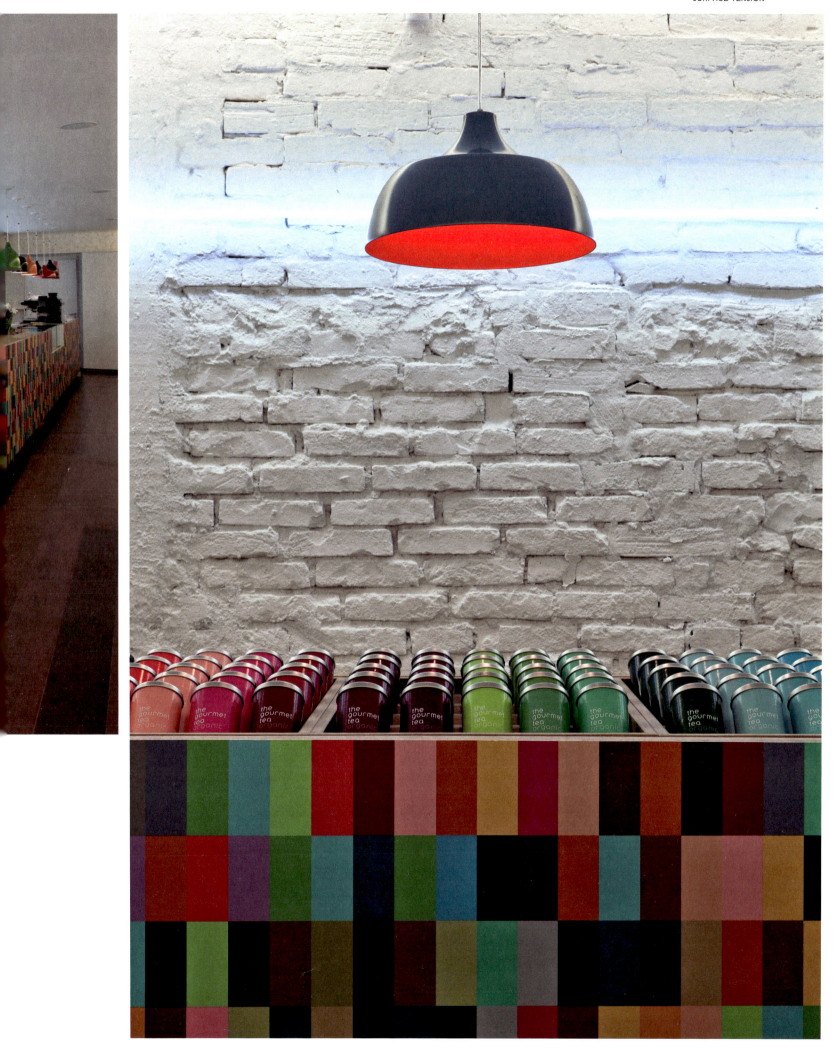

**Zukunfts-Licht
Light of the Future**

OLED-Licht wird zukünftig die Beleuchtung unserer Wohnungen und Häuser verändern: OLED-Lichtquellen können in Decken, Wände und sogar unsichtbar in Fenster integriert werden.

OLED light will revolutionize lighting in our homes. OLED light sources can be built into ceilings, walls and even integrated invisibly into windows.

BASF Future
2010 / Isle of Mainau, Germany

FLYING SAUCER, BASF SE
Client: BASF

During the Foundation Lindau Nobelprizewinners Meetings at Lake Constance in Germany, the chemical company BASF, together with the Isle of Mainau, participated in a group exhibition on the future of energy. Addressing the widest possible audience, the Berlin exhibition (or, as they phrase it, "attraction") designers Flying Saucer opted for an inviting, interactive presentation: They placed BASF research results and product innovations relating to gaining, storing, and using energy more efficiently in a large inflatable pavilion, with early prototypes and product samples showcased at its center. One of two interactive exhibits allowed visitors to experience what it takes to generate energy with their own body.

**Easy Shopping
Easy Shopping**

**Superschrauber
Super Screwdriver**

Elektronik
Electronics

**Lithium-Ionen-Batterien
Lithium Ion Batteries**

The Design Bar
2010 / Stockholm, Sweden

JONAS WAGELL
Client: Stockholm Furniture Fair

Swedish designer Wagell finished the bar and VIP area at the Stockholm Furniture Fair in 150 sheets of chipboard, 200 liters of paint, 350 square meters of carpet, and 300 colored balloons. Wagell made the most of the temporary nature of his assignment by creating an expressive space influenced by scenography and graphics rather than permanent architecture. Guests could eat light fare and enjoy a drink or coffee at the industry-themed bar, which pays homage to raw materials, craftsmanship, and refinement, which lie at the heart of furniture manufacturing. Wagell equipped the bar with his Montmartre furniture set made for Mitab, his Mr. Gardner outdoor easy chairs produced by Berga Form and his Cage steel baskets and Odd family of pendant lamps, bowls and vases for Hello Industry. The more secluded, less frequented VIP section resembled a forest that provided ground cover for more private meetings.

VIP LOUNGE
the forest

New York Minute, Artist Shop

2009 / Milan, Italy

ARCHITECTURE AT LARGE: RAFAEL DE CÁRDENAS

Client: Macro Future, Depart Foundation, Deitch Projects
See also pages 12, 46, 48, and 52

Curated by Kathy Grayson in collaboration with exhibition designer Rafael de Cárdenas, this 300-square-meter shop design was intended to be as artistic as the works of the 60 New York artists on show. For sponsors that included MACRO Future, DEPART Foundation, Deitch Projects and the City of Rome, New York-based Cárdenas constructed the retail space-cum-exhibition, with a life expectancy of three months, from nylon flagging, industrial shipping pallets, fluorescent duct tape, black balloons, La Repubblica newspapers, and black ribbon. The zines, stickers, T-shirts, jewelry, and books produced by the artists were framed by Cárdenas's brash lines and vociferous color palette in a festive but intimate, improvised space.

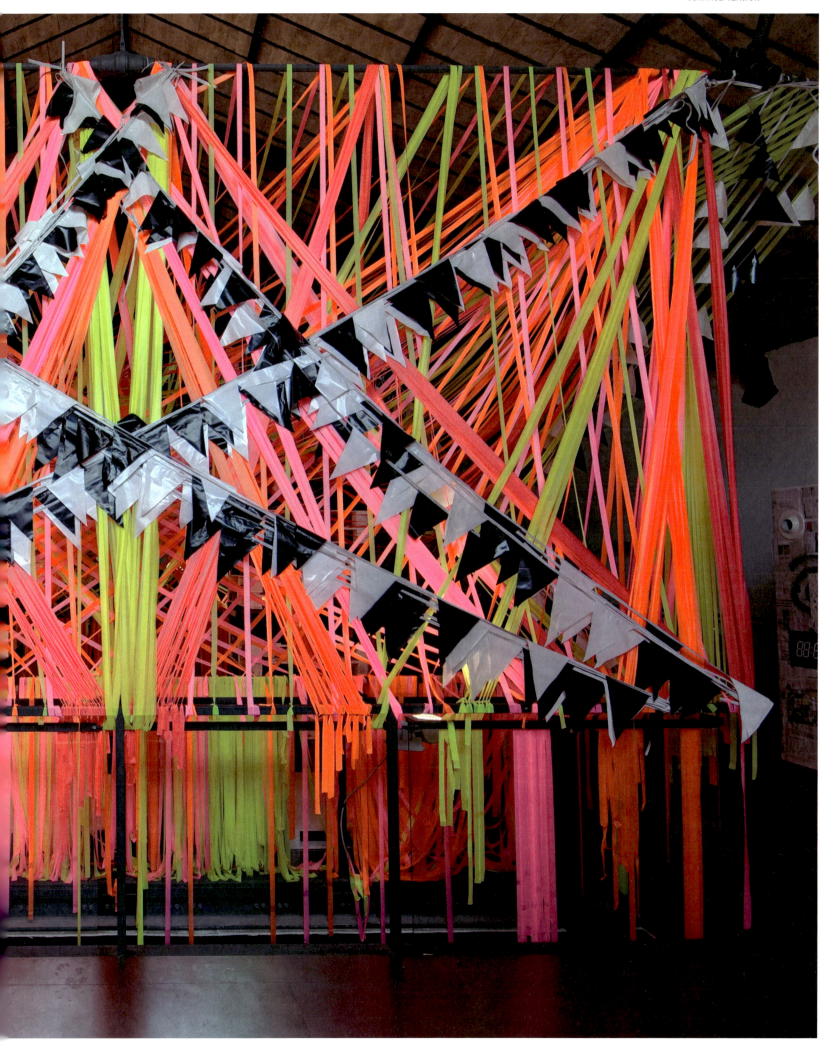

Wreck Center
2008 / New York, USA

ARCHITECTURE AT LARGE: RAFAEL DE CÁRDENAS
Client: Wreck Center
See also pages 12, 44, 48, and 52

In Manhattan, the Wreck Center played on the notion of the Rec (as in "recreation") Center, a supervised play space for kids. Local Architect at Large principal Rafael de Cárdenas designed a combination store, performance space, and art installation by covering the walls with graffiti, gold paint, and 5,800 feet of Day-GloTM masking tape. For a few months before the building containing the Wreck Center was torn down, downtown promoter Aaron "A-Ron" Bondaroff hosted a series of book signings, launch parties, concerts, stand-up comedy, and art exhibitions, selling products made by all the artists and performers involved.

Prism
Installation

2011 / London, UK

STUDIO XAG

Client: London Graphic Centre
See also pages 98 and 192

To create a spectacle at the entrance to the London Graphic Centre's flagship store in Covent Garden for six weeks, local studio XAG erected a 6-meter-high installation made from wire rope, acrylic, and hundreds of art supplies. Taking inspiration from the way in which light refracts through a prism, designers Xavier Sheriff and Gemma Ruse took over 100 hours to build it. The pair worked to maintain a feeling of lightness, ensure that it would be visually striking from all sides, and make the fixtures as discreet as possible. Laser-cut acrylic strips wired onto a taut steel rope held all the products, resulting in white and colored "rays" that seemed to "refract" from the smoked acrylic prism at its base.

OHWOW
Cappellini
2009 / New York, USA

ARCHITECTURE AT LARGE: RAFAEL DE CÁRDENAS
Client: OHWOW, Cappellini
See also pages 12, 44, 46, and 52

Former fashion designer, New York-based architect and designer Rafael de Cárdenas created a temporary shop-in-shop for progressive, multimedia art platform OHWOW inside Cappellini's flagship SoHo furniture showroom. Inspired by candy canes and gift wrap, Cárdenas's contrasting colors, Op Art lines, and choice of materials made the pocket-sized structure stand out robustly in an already colorful and visually crowded space. Customers are walked into a kaleidoscope of brightly-colored, industrial-strength cellophane, giving them the sensation of being inside an oversized gift. Stacked 1964 Bronzoni chairs from the Cappellini collection were also wrapped in colorful materials and served as pedestals for OHWOW publications from Ari Marcopoulos, Hanna Liden, Neck Face, and Rosson Crow, among others. Contemporary artists, among them Terrence Koh, Jim Drain, and Scott Campbell, were commissioned to create unique hand-painted holiday ornaments, which were on display and for sale on triangular towers outside the pop-up.

Reebok Flash
2008 / New York, USA

FORMAVISION
Client: Reebok

As visitors entered the Manhattan pop-up shop of British sportswear retailer Reebok, they were torn from three dimensions and dropped deliriously into two. Located for several weeks in a 1,000-square-meter former gallery, the shop sold flashy limited-edition sneakers and clothing designed in collaboration with a number of world-class artists. The geometric graphics and colorful distortion of every surface took their cues from multiple sources: the shoes, themselves; a camouflaging technique used on WWI "dazzle" war-ships; vorticsim, an early 20th-century English arts movement; and Reebok's halcyon decade, the 1980s, of which it has become a beloved symbol. The objects themselves served as graphic devices: Sculptural fixtures and seating were paired with stand-alone garment racks that appeared impossibly flat from certain angles and counters that tapered to a needlepoint. Formavision creative director Sebastien Agneessens felt free to eschew the benign colors and shapes, finer finishes, and lighting of a permanent store, opting instead for a Miami Vice clashiness that made the installation stand out in this crowded Manhattan retail district, generate heavy traffic, and reposition Reebok at the vanguard of the creative retail scene.

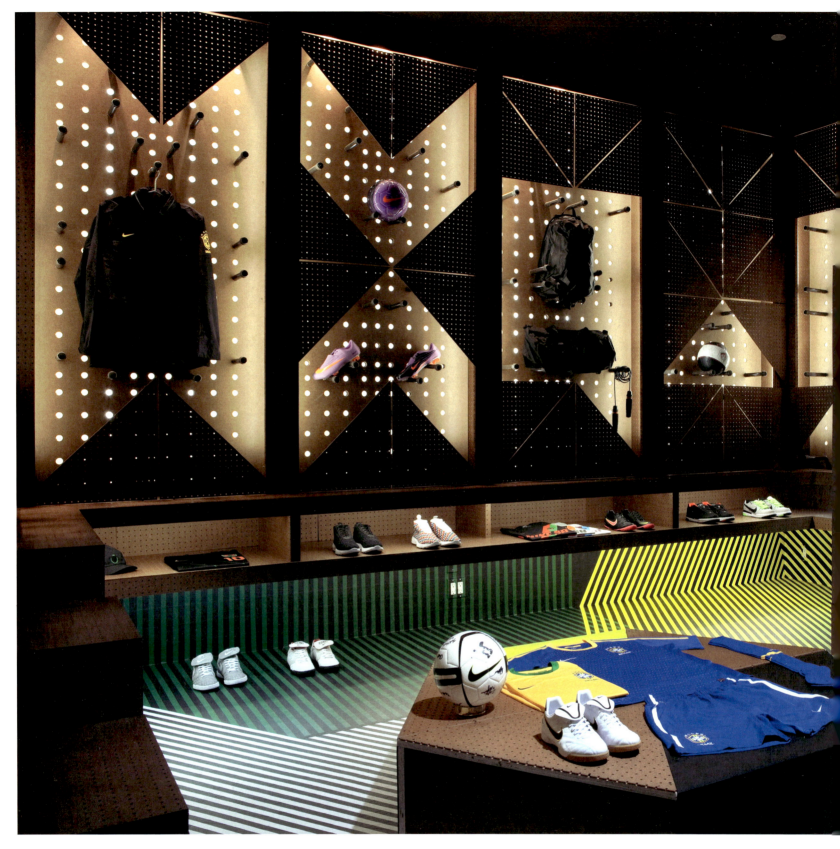

Nike Stadium NYC

2010 / New York, USA

ARCHITECTURE AT LARGE: RAFAEL DE CÁRDENAS

Client: Nike
See also pages 12, 44, 46, and 48

New York-based architect Rafael de Cárdenas's interior design for the temporary Nike Stadium in Manhattan coincided with the FIFA World Cup. Visitors to the 743-square-meter space were able to experience a world that featured not just sportswear and retail, but product design, film, photography, art, and music. The designer, who often uses everyday materials, worked utilitarian pegboard to create an elaborate effect. Under a directional, pitch-like pattern of linear fluorescent lights in the main event space, which was built to serve multiple functions, de Cárdenas dispersed polygonal modular cells throughout that visitors could move like players on a field. Depending on the event, the arrangement of the cells created micro-spaces for installation art, games, and other activities. De Cárdenas rotated and replicated a football pitch to create a unique pattern comprising directional lines and then applied this geometry to the floor using patterned tape to give it the latent energy of a sports stadium.

Dior Illustrated:
Réne Gruau
and the Line of
Beauty
2010 / London, UK

GITTA
GSCHWENDTNER
Client: Dior, Somerset House

For three months, timber and gauze were the materials used to showcase the work of Dior illustrator René Gruau, who drew some of the most iconic fashion images of the 20th century. London-based Gschwendtner's challenge was to create a compelling space from the unique architecture of the gallery for predominantly two-dimensional artworks. Her solution was simple: Gschwendtner built a series of timber frame boxes draped with sheer, gauze custom-dyed to complement the artifacts on show. In the main gallery, she staggered these diaphanous boxes in a pattern that loosely followed the profile of the room's vaulted ceiling.

Amicis Fashion Concept Store

2009 / Vienna, Austria

DENIS KOŠUTIĆ

Client: Amicis
See also pages 220 and 224

While designing an Amicis concept shop in Vienna, local architect Denis Košuti´c left vestiges of an existing hallway's demolition so that the corridor looks only roughly finished. Each of four adjacent, baroque rooms-within-the-room preserves its distinct ambience—Flower Power, Neo-Baroque, James Bond, and Boudoir—through the use of new, vintage, and bespoke fixtures and furniture, wallcoverings, fabrics, lighting and color schemes, in stark contrast to the crudeness of the corridor. Freestanding fitting rooms clad entirely in mirror interrupt the sightlines between and amongst the shop's four rooms-within-a-room, giving the shop an additional textured visual layer.

Snog Chelsea
2010 / London, UK

CINIMOD STUDIO
Client: Snog Pure Frozen Yogurt

This frozen yogurt shop features the bold color scheme and robust forms that one might expect from a former Future Systems architect who has experimented extensively with digital lighting design. Using the product itself, the company's branding (by Ico Design), and the cheeky name "snog" as starting points the design concept abstracts a "perpetual British summer," with "grass" floors, floral graphics, and an undulating digital-sky ceiling that varies in depth and pitch and was fabricated from CNC-milled mirrored panels with a stretch ceiling diffuser. Each of the light ribbons contains a ladder grid of bespoke, individually controlled RGBW LED battens (the addition of white to the RGB spectrum sharpening color accuracy). The amBX lighting technology generates complex effects with minimal programming, and allows the digital sky to ripple with color shifts in a real-time response to the store's music system.

WOOD WOOD
Double Denim Pop-Up Shop-in-Shop
2010 / Hamburg, Germany

GARY SUMMER, YBDPT STUDIO
Client: WOOD WOOD

Using wood, logo tape, and vinyl stickers and taking cues from the brand's double denim range, YBDPT Studio designed a window installation for this two-month Hamburg retail space by applying white stripes to the storefront, generating visual complexity from rudimentary graphic elements. The interior hosted an installation by Berlin-based artist Gary Summer, who wove together wooden panels covered with WOOD WOOD logo-tape to create a display for the denim apparel.

Catwalk
2007 / Frankfurt-Main, Germany

FRANKEN ARCHITEKTEN GMBH
Client: BMW Group

MINI launched its Clubman car in a 1,200-square-meter trade fair booth at the International Motor Show (IAA) 2007. The cubical booth, which alluded to the car's dimensions, combined elements of art, fashion, and nightclubbing to appeal to "the trendsetters from post-modern milieus," who are the car's target customer. The Frankfurt/Main-based architects referenced the fashion industry through the softening use of textiles: fabric-covered facades and a felt-covered floor and seating systems, as well as garments draped on illuminated hangers. Two interactive audio-visual media walls flanked the stage inside, looping images of artwork, surreal figures, and graphic devices that were controlled in real time by a video jockey with live feeds of material shot on-site, in the booth's Blue Box.

LICENCE TO FILL.
MINI ONE CLUBMAN.

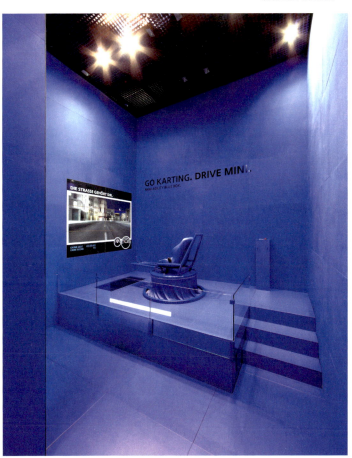

GO KARTING. DRIVE MINI.
MINI AGILITY BLUE BOX.

FOR GUYS WHO HAVE
MORE THAN CARS ON THEIR MIND.
MINI COLLECTION 2007/2008.

MINI COLLECTION EYEWEAR.

CLUBMAN TO WEAR.
MINI COLLECTION 2007/2008.

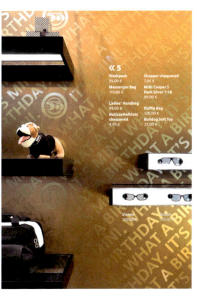

Dutch Masters, Schiphol Museum Shop
2010 / Amsterdam, Netherlands

UXUS
Client: Schiphol
See also pages 230 and 241

Shoppers walk into a canvas on entering the Schiphol airport shop of the Netherlands' renowned fine art institution, the Rijksmuseum. The shop offers visitors the opportunity to view the work of the Old Dutch Masters while purchasing masterpieces of contemporary Dutch design to take home with them. They navigate the retail space and its product range along a three-dimensional timeline of the tiny nation's outsized creativity, from the "Golden Age" of painting to the "Concept Age" of modern design. As one proceeds, the interior graduates from the golden hues of the 17th century to gray tones representing today. A vast three-dimensional representation of Vermeer's *The Milk Maid* and a self-portrait of Rembrandt allow the store to stand out elegantly against the industrial chilliness of the terminal.

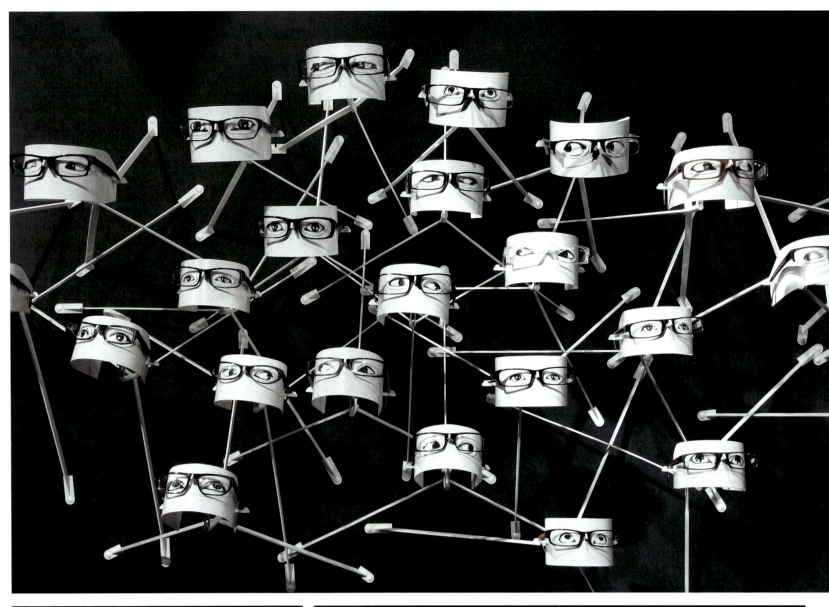

[1]

[2]

[1] **Kirk Originals**
2010 / London UK

[2] **Dunhill**
2010 / New York, USA

CAMPAIGN

Client: [1] Kirk Originals [2] Dunhill

Tasked to create a one-week installation to preview Dunhill's luxury mens' Fall / Winter 2010-11 collection and a range of limited-edition merchandise during New York Fashion Week, Campaign "imported" the brand's London headquarters and the former home of Alfred Dunhill. They recreated the Georgian-style Bourdon House in a disused warehouse in the Meatpacking District with its ethereal facade. To do so, they suspended lasercut white powder-coated aluminum panels from the ceiling using unistruts to allow them to hover dramatically above the black rubber floor. A true-to-scale exterior and its Mayfair surroundings was printed on vinyl and illuminated theatrically with photographic lights. The interior featured vintage furniture from Dunhill's archive, 30 key looks on bespoke easels, frames, and antique brass clothes rails, and a mirror above the fireplace that served as a canvas on which to project a film of the latest Dunhill Paris presentation. Through projections, guests were able to sit on park benches in a modern interpretation of an English memorial garden. The exhibition ended in a pop-up shop and events space with a minimal monochromatic look that formed a contemporary emblem while showcasing the progressive character of the historical brand.

Raise Your Game
2010 / London, UK

WILSON BROTHERS
Client: Nike, NSW
See also page 182

A black-box retail installation lined with neon tubing by the Wilson Brothers for Nike's East London 1948 space served as the weekly meeting place for RUN-DEM-CREW, a local urban running club. The dark floor covering called Nike GRIND was a 100% recycled rubber sport surface, a minimum of 10% of which consists of the soles of recycled training shoes—900 pairs went into the 120-square-meter club. The "Running Man" floor graphic incorporated the markings of three maps used by the the runners, red (5k), yellow (8k), and green (10k) routes in a color scheme that also gave a visual tip of the hat to club founder Charlie Dark's weekly Reggae running podcasts. The line width matched traditional sports pitch markings while "X" marked the 1948 space on the London map. A set of 12 modular units—alluding to the tiered stadium or grandstand seating common to most spectator sports— formed the display system. The steel and laminated plywood units ran on wheels for easy mobility. Equally useful as table-top displays, or auditorium seating for events, set back-to-back the stepped units recalled a classic winners' podium. Detachable, multi-positional hanging rails echoed the goal posts dotting nearby Hackney Marshes. A 6×8 meter neon football pitch installation hung horizontally from the ceiling, dominated by a NESW compass, which contained the letters of the Nike Sports Wear brand initials, as well as the 1948 East London location.

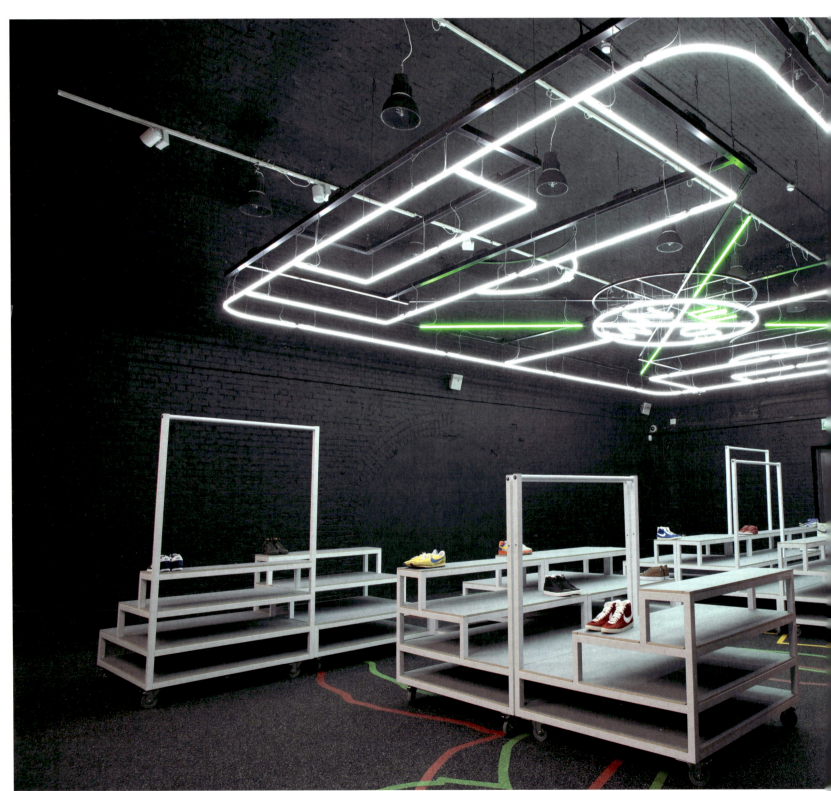

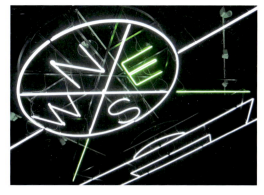

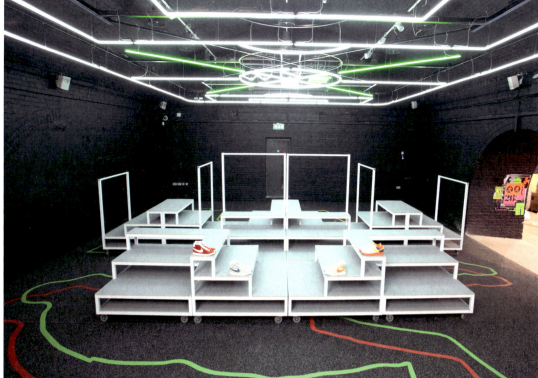

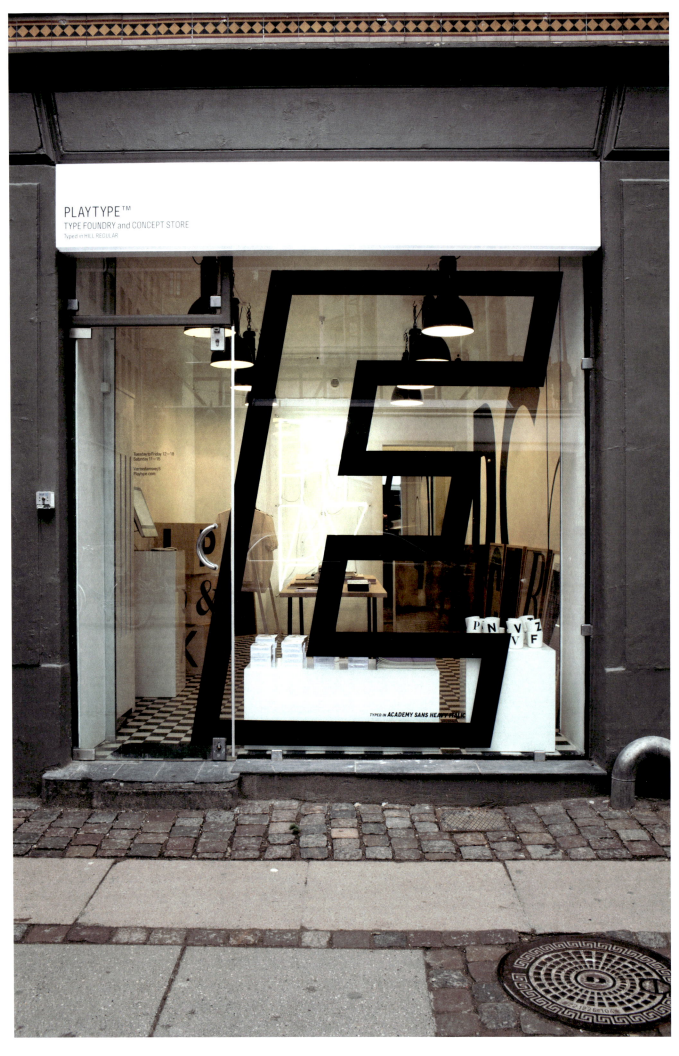

Playtype
Concept Store
2010 / Copenhagen, Denmark

E-TYPES
Client: Playtype Concept Store

The world's first bricks-and-mortar type foundry hung its shingle in Copenhagen for one year, a concept shop rendition of one of Europe's foremost online font shops, playtype.com. Its walls dotted with letters in various typefaces, the boutique stocked more than 100 fonts by London-based typographers A2/SW/HK and e-Types, the 15-year-old agency known for designing fonts for the likes of Carlsberg, Aquascutum, Georg Jensen, and the National Gallery of Denmark, among others. Walk-in customers purchased fonts loaded onto specially designed USB sticks that looked like credit cards, as well as products and editions such as t-shirts, posters, notebooks. Even after the shop closes, it will be possible to buy the products online.

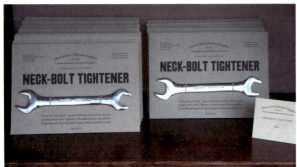

Hoxton Street Monster Supplies
2010 / London, UK

WE MADE THIS
Client: Hoxton Street Monster Supplies

Hoxton Street Monster Supplies is the shopfront for the Ministry of Stories, a pioneering children's writing workshop in London that sells "bespoke and everyday items for the living, dead and undead" and is meant to be an embodiment of the imagination, as if visitors were walking into a storybook. Display shelves even hide a secret door, through which children access the classroom.

ONLY ONE
GIANT
IN THE SHOP
AT A TIME

·

CUSTOMERS
ARE POLITELY
REQUESTED
TO REFRAIN
FROM EATING
THE STAFF

·

NOCTURNAL
OPENING
(BY APPOINTMENT)
FOR VAMPIRE
CUSTOMERS
ONLY

BEANS
(MAGIC OR
OTHERWISE)
ARE NOT
ACCEPTED
AS PAYMENT

·

HUMANS
WELCOME,
BUT ENTIRELY
AT THEIR
OWN RISK

·

ANGRY MOBS
PLEASE DOUSE
YOUR TORCHES
BEFORE ENTERING
THE SHOP

All That Matters

Linoleum, cardboard tubes, shipping pallets, thousands of white pencils, and plain white shopping bags: Highbrow or low, material can convey mood and personalilty and sometimes it shapes the space instead of the space shaping it.

Materials may simply determine the look-and-feel of an interior and brand, but at other times, the material is the message. In Tel Aviv's **Delicatessen** boutiques, linoleum and pegboard invert the expensive and lengthy architectural process, instead mimicking the much less costly, ephemerally quick process of fashion design. Through the most minimal of materials, **Zucker** is suggesting that, to thrive, architecture needs to honor the manipulation of the material over the material itself, design over its rote execution, the idea over the object.

Today, salvaging, recycling, or recontextualizing materials is the planet-friendly thing to do and it is being done better. Using waste panels from which they cut their CNC-milled ply sheet furniture to create partitions and stair railings in the **Droog** New York store, **Studio Makkink & Bey** demonstrated that sustainability can also be aesthetically sustainable. But it is not done in blind service to the green trend; instead designers, consumers, and companies are recognizing the beauty and utility of objects that carry histories and individual memories through time.

March Studio's shops for Australian cosmetics brand **Aesop** are built from a sustainable but banal material—the company's own packaging—and made extraordinary through its repetition. March netted, sliced, stacked, and staggered thousands of bare brown cardboard boxes to create sculptural walls, ceilings, display surfaces, and even a chandelier.

The exaggerated application of a single material can design an emotional experience. **Snarkitecture** whittled through an entire freight container stuffed with Styrofoam to create a cave-like temporary fashion boutique, making the monolithic ubiquity of the material the source of shoppers' experience of the brand as a sanctuary for creativity. **Tokujin Yoshioka** built a frozen ice storm around his transparent **Kartell** furniture collection, made from floating drifts of sheer, white-tinged plastic prism sticks to evoke natural phenomena, impalpable or invisible to the human eye. This is a brand, the installation implied, that is engaging in culture, not just commerce. Materials are the not just the clay that gives form to our ideas; sometimes they, themselves, contain the ideas that give form to our experience.

Hermès Rive Gauche
2010 / Paris, France

RENA DUMAS ARCHITECTURE INTERIEURE
Client: Hermès

Hermès switched sides, opening a three-story, 2,155-square-meter fashion and housewares boutique, tea room, bookstore, and florist on Paris' Left Bank after 170 years on the Right. Rehabilitated and re-designed by RDAI, 17 Rue de Sèvres is a former Art Deco hotel swimming pool containing three lantern- or seed-like 9-meter-high pods made from woven ashwood. A fourth pod connects the staircase to a (dry) pool filled with mosaic tiles. Over-head, the theme of water continues as, thanks to projections connected to the lighting system, its reflection seems to play across the ceiling.

Lignumpavillon
2009 / *Various locations*

FREI + SAARINEN ARCHITEKTEN
Client: Lignum, Holzwirtschaft Schweiz

Basel-based Frei and Saarinen used 8 tons and 541 CNC-milled cuts of wood to build a sculptural pavilion and exhibition space that would be used 10 times through 2012. As the name suggests, Lignum is the Swiss information center responsible for all things wood. The center wanted a space that could demonstrate a contemporary architectural use of the material. The resulting structure comprised 20 layers of 50 mm-thick planes and vertical elements 130 mm in height on which visitors can walk. Like a pixelated image, the layers form a path that leads them in the shape of a figure eight.

Karis
2007 / Hiroshima, Japan

SUPPOSE DESIGN OFFICE:
MAKOTO TANIJIRI, KAZUTAKA SUMI
Client: Ka.zu.in Ltd.

For client Ka.Zu.In Ltd., Suppose designed a 118-square-meter boutique and event space in a Hiroshima shopping center using cardboard tubes. By moving through the space, the visitor's perspective changes completely, much as it might in a natural limestone cavern lined with stalactites. The designers layered the tubes randomly so as to create uneven surfaces and arches that serve as irregular partitions for the store. This simultaneously simple complexity also makes the space suitable for various uses and events throughout the year.

UDK Bookshop
2009 / Berlin, Germany

UDK BOOKSHOP:
DALIA BUTVIDAITE, LEONARD STEIDLE, JOHANNES DRECHSLER
Client: UDK Berlin

On a shoestring budget of € 2,000, this three-day university bookshop was designed by a group of competition-winning architecture, art, and graphic design students. The scheme focused on cardboard because of its flexibility, stability and affordability, but also because it expresses impermanence, lightness, and sustainability.
The designers cut, perforated, folded, and glued together 600 2.6 x 1.3 meter corrugated cardboard panels to form a monolithic block, which they then pulled apart like a giant accordian to give it its final shape as a display wall. Adaptable to any space, the unit can be folded down to a tenth of its length for storage or transport while the cardboard is load-bearing enough to not only hold books, but also to serve as a bench. The unit transformed a rectangular room both visually and by imposing new ways for visitors to circulate the space. At the end of the event, it was auctioned off to provide funding for subsequent publications and next year's bookshop.

15,000 Pencils - Fair Booth for Mitteldeutscher Verlag Publishers
2010 / Leipzig, Germany

STABE ALBERT GESTALTUNG

Client: Mitteldeutscher Verlag
See also page 186

Using thousands of branded pencils stuck into perforated walls, interior architect Albert and book designer Stabe designed an exhibition booth to be used annually for six years at the Leipzig Book Fair in Germany by Mitteldeutscher Verlag Publishers. Visitors were free to take a pencil with them, knowing that they would be dismantling the booth by doing so, or they could simply reposition pencils in the perforated grid as they wished. The designers turned a rudimentary but versatile writing utensil into a three-dimensional pattern that acted as both bookshelves and lettering. Some of the 15,000 pencils were even used as building components: 315 pencils held eight perforated boards in position.

Paperbag Igloo
2008 / Tokyo, Japan

YASUTAKA YOSHIMURA ARCHITECTS
Client: Morioka Shoten

Morioka Shoten, the renowned and historical secondhand Tokyo artbook store, Yoshimura's office created a temporary exhibition space. For two weeks, an igloo assembled from the white paper shopping bags used by the shop created a modern moment within the historical building. By stacking the bags closely and taping their string handles together, the architects made this inner "room" darker while creating a display board of sorts on the interior. This made it possible to project photographs from Yoshimura's book, *Super Legal Buildings* here. Following the exhibition, the bags were returned to their original purpose for use as shopping bags.

Artshop 10
2010 / Basel, Switzerland

ZMIK
Client: Sevensisters
See also page 32

A 112-square-meter temporary design boutique mounted for one week during Art 41 Basel for Swiss brand Sevensisters was designed by local design firm ZMIK from plywood and lashing straps. ZMIK stacked plywood crates and bound them with lashings into parcels that could be strung together in a sequence to form a terraced product display. The crates also offered space for storage, accessed from the side of each pallet. This storage space remained visible but visually subordinate to the well-illuminated display surfaces. Limited-edition Artbags, the shop's bestseller, served as wallcoverings and, as they were sold, gradually cleared the walls of any ornamentation, and ensored that the appearance of the shop changed constantly.

9 Department Store & Gallery
2010 / Fukuoka, Japan

KOICHI FUTATSUMATA
Client: Alohanine Co.,Ltd
See also page 146

This boutique interior in Fukuoka, Japan was designed by Koichi Futatsumata to be used as a shop, gallery, or event space. Since the main use of the space is retail, however, the key fixture became an adaptable, readymade display rack. To make the rack easily reconfigurable to additional uses the designer repurposed inexpensive off-the-shelf rails typically used in factories or warehouses. He also made it easy to remove and store the shelving units and additional bespoke components such as mirrors and hangers.

BAERCK
2010 / Berlin, Germany

LLOT LLOV
Client: BAERCK

Design studio llot llov chose not to finish the wood used in the 140-square-meter BAERCK fashion boutique, but combined it with white surfaces and mirrors to support the style of the different labels and pieces. Mobile display trolleys—inspired by the forms of vehicles from various eras used to transport BAERCK merchandise to Berlin—allow clerks to change the appearance of the shop regularly.

Delicatessen
Clothing Store

2006 / Tel Aviv, Israel

Z-A: GUY ZUCKER

Client: Idit Barak
See also page 116

By cutting, folding, rolling, stacking, and wrapping linoleum and cardboard tubes, New York designer Zucker has transformed off-the-shelf materials into something couture. Zucker dressed the 84-square-metre fashion boutique in a "garment" that serves as the store's furniture: display racks, a fitting room, a cash desk and storefront. Because this garment can be easily replaced, the interior architecture keeps pace with the mercurial fashion industry. A second virtue? The entire project cost a mere $3,000, and materials accounted for only a third of it.

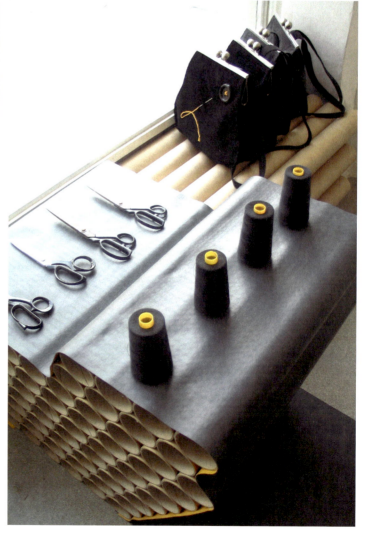

QWSTION
The Wallpaper
2010 / Zurich, Switzerland

AEKAE
Client: QWSTION

Zurich- and London-based Aeberhard and Kaegi designed a luggage collection for Swiss fashion brand Qwstion in 2008 followed by a shop interior that uses the product itself to create display systems. Here, the collection was used to "paper" the walls in monolithic fields of color with the backpacks, bags, and duffles lending the surfaces texture and depth. Aekae describe their work as clear and simple and, through repetition, give the already handsome, minimalist pieces added impact. Just like the bags, the interior was built for function but given a distinctive look.

Coven Store
2011 / Belo Horizonte, Brazil

MARCELO ALVARENGA

Client: Coven

The first shop for Brazilian knitwear label Coven involved the conversion of a two-story brick house in Belo Horizonte, Brazil. Dressed in a metallic mesh "garment" that itself appears to be knit, the facade suggests woven yarn, knitwear's "raw material," and can be repainted every season. A glazed pergola on the ground floor penetrates the mesh facade and draws natural light into the shop. Artists Susana Bastos and Ana Vaz created a permanent in-store display of fabric and vine-like braided ropes for the 160-square-meter interior, using thread and surplus material.

Rolls
2011 / Tokyo, Japan

SINATO:
CHIKARA OHNO, KEN KAMADA
Client: Diesel Japan Co.,Ltd.
See also page 148

Aluminum: thin and easily bent by hand, yet tougher than cloth or paper, created the simultaneously hard and soft character of Sinato's installation in the Aoyama Diesel Denim Gallery in Tokyo for Diesel Japan. By unfurling or winding a single long strip of aluminum into spools, the designers generated a sculptural field of display surfaces from the entrance to the rear of the shop. Layered or in a single sheet, the material's strength increased and decreased, making its function and features change as well. The flexible quality of the material became a notional alloy that united the suppleness of garments and the durability of architecture.

Blueprint
2009 / New York, USA

STUDIO MAKKINK & BEY
Client: Droog Design

The New York shop for Amsterdam design collective Droog sold edition furniture and accessories in a space where even display cases and other interior architectural elements were for sale. Rotterdam designers Rian Makkink and Juergen Bey allowed salespeople to reconfigure the layout of the store themselves by moving sheer curtains with pixellated graphics along ceiling tracks to create diverse partitions. The shop's designers also made coffee tables and chairs routed from flat panels and used the off-cuts to construct walls and a balustrade leading downstairs. A half-scale home that was CNC-milled from lightweight blue polyurethane foam, complete with climbing ivy, a working chimney, and a picket fence, anchored the space and could be purchased in six cross sections or customized as a whole to suit any interior. It was a microarchitecture-within-architecture that created an environment for the products while becoming a product itself. The store suggested that Droog is a brand able to design, not just fill, interiors.

Gaggenau
Living Kitchen

2011 / Cologne, Germany

EINS:33

Client: Gaggenau,
BSH Home Appliances Pte Ltd.

Eins:33 built a six-day, 310-square-meter trade fair booth in Cologne for kitchen appliance giant Gaggenau. To illustrate the brand identity—authentic, uncompromising, and extraordinary—the Munich-based studio created an artfully modified factory environment in which visitors could enjoy a glimpse of the company's high-quality fabrication process in three zones: production, experience (of the appliances), and luxury. A 5-meter-high construction of IPE steel and glass profiles held the 15-meter-long company logo, an artifact of the original Gaggenau factory, while acrylic boxes gave visitors a peek behind-the-scenes and displayed technical details of the products. Nearby, a stack of massive oak planks served as a wine tasting bar.

Wut Rooms
2009 / Berlin, Germany
RYOKO ANDO
Client: H.P. France S.A., WUT Berlin

With a three-day lifespan, interior designer Ryoko Ando's cardboard, timber, and tape pop-up shop for H.P.France/

Wut Berlin extended the German multi-brand boutique's reach to Room 2009, the first of Tokyo's two biannual fashion weeks. Ando divided the retail floor into seven brand areas and combined the notions of kindergarten and labyrinth as a basis for her raw and childlike 93-square-meter space. Her low-tech approach stemmed from memories of constructing secret fortresses from found materials as a child.

The Goodhood Store

2010 / London, UK

THE GOODHOOD STORE FOUNDERS:
JO SINDLE,
KYLE STEWART
Client: The Goodhood Store

London's 500-square-meter Goodhood clothing shop, designed by its owners, is a collage of salvaged wood, Perspex, powder-coated metal, and spray-painted bespoke cabinets. A mix of old and new, worn and smooth, dark and bright, it incorporates the work of local artists, including Word to Mother who made the wooden structures, Lucas Price who created the lightbox messages, and Russell Maurice and Dan Sparkes who did a collection of hidden doors.

A
SELECTION
OF
GOODS
ROOTED
IN
DESIGN
QUALITY
AND
CREATIVITY

Clouds
2009 / London, UK

STUDIO XAG
Client: Diesel
See also pages 47 and 192

To create an indoor installation for a one-day Diesel press event, local Studio XAG produced 100 clouds made from polyester wadding and monofilament, and filled the 1,000-square-meter London space with them, from the storefront up a corridor and throughout the sunlit showroom.

Aktipis Flowershop
2008 / Patras, Greece

POINT SUPREME ARCHITECTS
Client: Aktipis Flowershop

Is this 40-square-meter flower shop in Patras, Greece located indoors or out? To create the display, Point Supreme clad 14 archetypical tables, which vary in proportion and size and can be grouped and combined in diverse ways, with square, white tiles. They then scaled the wallpaper pattern, a blurry glimpse of jungle vegetation, to gigantic size. Images of birds, taken from an old Greek encyclopedia, appear to be playing with the interior's technical details: plugs, water drains, and speakers. The facade incorporates a salvaged steel door and embossed leaf-pattern glass; a section of it is set back, providing a display surface outside the shop. Garden chairs used inside, small plastic lizards on the tables, and the twitter of birds emanating from the speakers, round out a surreal experience.

Men at Work Brugge
2006 / Bruges, Belgium

BEARANDBUNNY
Client: Men at Work
See also page 150

Bearandbunny were smitten with the worn-out character of a 500-square-meter former carpet showroom in Bruges when they were asked to transform it into a shop for Belgian clothier Men at Work. The designers preserved most existing elements but drafted them into service in new and, at times, exaggerated ways. Radiators became display fittings; clamp lamps became small-goods displays; old paving tiles clad the cash counter and floor. In an old storage room the designers discovered sliding walls and turned them into fitting rooms. Old-fashioned plush velvet armchairs were dispersed throughout the space and, along with the original lathed ceiling and strip-lighting, a smattering of succulents and two canaries (who produced canary chicks six weeks after the opening), the shop radiates tasteful coziness and provides interactive fun for visitors.

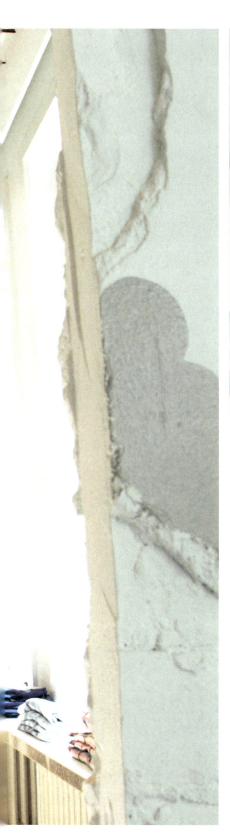

Lulamae
2009 / Melbourne, Australia

BREATHE ARCHITECTURE
Client: Lulamae

The designers Breath, from Brunswick, Australia used 100% post consumer waste recycled cardboard to prefabricate the Melbourne fashion boutique Lulamae. The sustainable design for this two-month pop-up started with the streetscape of the brand's original shop, which was then romanticised as if it were the enchanted setting of a fairytale. Built at a slightly small scale, it allowed shoppers to feel larger than life. Cardboard tubes served as columns and hanging rails. Another happy ending: The printed laser-cut panels that formed the storefronts were shipped flat packed to the site where they were folded and snapped together in a single day and disassembly took only two hours.

Papercut

2007 / Athens, Greece

ELINA
DROSSOU

Client: Eleftheriades Yiorgos –
Yeshop in House

The low-cost, site-specific design of
this 90-square-meter Athens shop for
client Eleftheriades Yiorgos synthe-
sized fashion and architecture. Existing
furniture was rearranged, repurposed,
and anchored to eco-friendly, hand-cut
sheets of cardboard, glued together
layer by layer. Tables attached to the
wall and lit from behind served as
lamps. Bookshelves turned sideways
and mounted to the wall became displays. Opposite, a biomorphic element,
inspired, like the garments for sale,
by the human body and consisting of
thousands of sheets of corrugated cardboard was "accessorized" with boxes and
used to display accessories.

[1] Aesop Merci
2010 / Paris, France

[2] Aesop Flinders Lane
2008 / Melbourne, Australia

MARCH STUDIO
Client: Aesop
See also page 236

March Studio's eighth shop for Australian cosmetic brand Aesop took the form of a pop-up shop that colonized the Paris department store Merci for three months. Tasked to create an organic, flowing space, the designers captured 4,500 cardboard shipper boxes, boxes actually used by Aesop to ship their product worldwide, in a 40-square-meter net to form a continuous wall and ceiling feature. The project continues the studio's success in elevating everyday objects through repetition and in giving their materials a second life: All of the boxes were reused after the shop was shuttered, shipped out to customers through Aesop's mail order system.

To create the Flinders Lane Melbourne location for Australian cosmetics brand Aesop, for five days, the architects at March Studio folded and stacked 3,000 industrial-grade cardboard product packaging. Sturdy, practical, and visually compatible with the merchandise, cardboard forms the serving counter, display shelves, and eastern wall of the store. The interior, constructed initially to be temporary, communicates the company's longstanding interest in innovative design and has earned such high praise from the public that it may not be dismantled at all. In the event that it is, however, the cardboard will be reused—for its original purpose—to package Aesop elixirs.

[2]

[1] **Shortcut**
2007 / Chiba, Japan

[2] **Foundation**
2006 / Hyogo, Japan

RYUJI NAKAMURA
Client: JIN Co.,Ltd.

Both stores designed for Jin Company by Nakamura showcase eyewear without resorting to the cumbersome glass cabinets so typical of most optical shops. The 104-square-meter Shortcut store is situated in a large shopping mall, and as it consists only of passages people tend to enter the shop to take a shortcut. On their way, they can try on glasses displayed like a wallpaper pattern on the unusually tall walls, all the while feeling as comfortable as fish gliding through a coral reef.

The eyewear sold in the Foundation store is displayed on low concrete walls resembling the foundations of a house. Accompanying accessories are laid out on wooden furniture placed among the concrete walls.

Richard Chai Boutique

2010 / New York, USA

SNARKITECTURE

Client: Richard Chai

Brooklyn-based art and architecture office Snarkitecture built a 44-square-meter boutique with an expiration date of five days on a budget of $5000 during the Building Fashion event in Manhattan. Tasked by fashion designer Richard Chai to present his clothes through an interactive and "emotional" shopping experience, Snarkitecture "built" the shop through a process of subtraction. They filled a converted construction trailer with blocks of EPS foam and then carved them out with custom-built wire cutters, leaving wide striations. Shoppers entered an organic world—the crevasse of a glacier, perhaps— contained within an industrial shell. Installation took three days and disassembly 45 minutes, after which the material was returned to the manufacturer for recycling.

Delicatessen Clothing Store
2009 / Tel Aviv, Israel

Z-A: GUY ZUCKER
Client: Idit Barak
See also page 84

When the Delicatessen fashion boutique—whose first location celebrated humble linoleum as a chic finish—opened its second Tel Aviv installment, it made a star of pegboard instead. On a $10,000 budget, New York architect Guy Zucker of Z-A lined the two-story, 34-square-meter shop with custom-perforated white hardboard. The interior deliberately aligns architecture and fashion, using cheap materials with sophistication to make the crude, off-the-(hardware-store)-shelf material resemble a lace gown. Hooks in the walls serve as display and, when bare, as ornament, as do the furnishings, which appear to be cut from the pegboard pattern and, when lifted off the wall in spots, reveal their lemon-yellow "lingerie."

Arnsdorf
Concept Store

2011 / Melbourne, Australia

EDWARDS MOORE
Client: Arnsdorf

The women's fashion label created by the Australian fashion designer Jade Sarita Arnott includes the Opticks collection, inspired by crystals and prismatic effects. To build the Arnsdorf concept store, which did business for three days in the Melbourne suburb of Fitzroy, local designers Edwards Moore were inspired by the signature faceted print of the clothing range, other crystalline structures, and even Superman's shard-like Fortress of Solitude. Unexpectedly, however, they translated these sharp, angular images into a superlatively soft interior, webbed with stretched hosiery in shades ranging from pastels to nudes, corals, and earthy browns.

Mortal Coil
2006 / New York, USA

URBAN A&O
Client: BOFFO, Architizer

Urban A&O was one of several winners of the BOFFO/Architizer-sponsored competition to create a two-week retail installation for a partner fashion designer in a cargo container that formerly housed a real estate sales office in Manhattan's Chelsea neighborhood west of the High Line Park. Their collaborator was couture milliner Heather Huey for whom they installed a display wall of high-density foam and textile that undulated in striated black waves to showcase Huey's avant-garde designs.

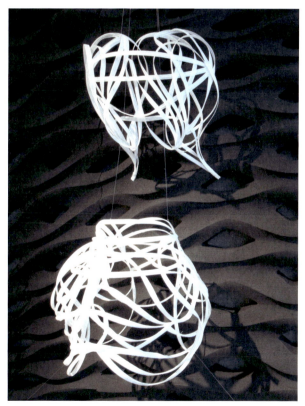

Romanticism 2
2007 / Hangzhou, China

SKSK ARCHITECTS:
KEIICHIRO SAKO,
TAKESHI ISHIZAKA
Client: Langmanyishen Limited Company
See also pages 8 and 26

Like clothing, space wraps the body. Beijing-based SKSK dressed the 1,142-square-meter interior of the Hangzhou outpost of Chinese fashion franchise Romanticism 2 with a net-like, biomorphic structure that defines floor, wall, and ceiling, and serves as partitions, banisters, counters, and furniture. The distribution of the oil-painted epoxy resin, steel rod, styrofoam, and glass fiber net creates the impression it has been absorbed through the facade into the shop interiors. To increase the drama, illumination, and illusion of greater volume, the first floor ceiling was sheathed with curved, mirror-finished stainless steel. Objects reflected in it appear to be floating in water—where the sky should be.

The Invisibles by Tokujin Yoshioka
2010 / Milan, Italy

TOKUJIN YOSHIOKA
Client: Kartell

Yoshioka presented his The Invisibles collection in Kartell's Milan flagship store for a week during the Milan Furniture Fair. The Tokyo-based designer's interior installation, made from an accretion of sheer, white-tinged plastic prism sticks, was inspired by natural phenomena and unseen elements such as wind and light. "The presence of the object is eradicated," said Yoshioka, who left visitors with the impression that they were walking into a snowflake—or a modern refinement of Superman's Fortress of Solitude.

Life Will Kill You
2010 / West Hollywood, USA

SPORTS
Client: Revolve Clothing

This interior concept investigated the razor's edge between aggression and elegance by using everyday industrial materials that have dark applications and provided high contrast with the West Hollywood boutique's sleek fashions. Sports used plastic zip ties and lamp cord to build and bind Life Will Kill You, a temporary 46-square-meter, $2000 showroom installation for Los Angeles-based Revolve Clothing. Woven together, more than 100,000 zip ties formed a floating textile volume that nestled beneath an existing soffit. The exterior of this volume was faced with longer, wider, white zip ties while the interior featured shorter, finer multicolored ones. The resulting form served as an accessory to the black-and-white-garbed shop interior, offering ever-changing glimpses of vivid color combinations as shoppers moved around it.

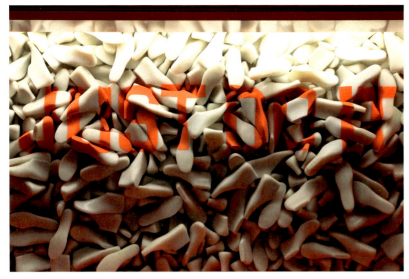

Nike Harajuku
2009 / Tokyo, Japan
WONDERWALL INC.
Client: Nike
See also page 22

Masamichi Katayama's design of the first Nike flagship in Tokyo features the largest NIKEiD Studio in Japan and was imagined as a 945-square-meter playing field that would be accessible to both serious athletes and recreational sports enthusiasts alike. The main entrance was placed off-center to encourage smoother circulation and exploration. Encased in glass with vibration finish stainless steel, a staircase leads to the second floor, crowned with a huge chandelier consisting of various styles of all-white Nike sneakers. An adjacent wooden shelving unit is backed with a collage of the waffle molds traditionally used to manufacture running shoes. Inspired by the old-school American-style gymnasium, the design of the second floor NIKEiD and Nike Sportswear areas lead to the iD Private room, which hosts the NIKEiD by-appointment-only program, and is enclosed in patterned curved glass. Past a circular display case, an unobtrusive spiral staircase leads up to the third floor, which is dedicated to football and features a vitrine of chaotically piled shoe molds.

NIKE1LOVE
2007 / Tokyo, Japan

TORAFU ARCHITECTS:
KOICHI SUZUNO, SHINYA KAMURO
Client: Nike Japan Corp.

This 108-square-meter Nike Air Force 1 store was built in Harajuku with an expiration date of one year. The plan was to enable customers to watch as the edition of Air Force 1s increased by displaying the growing collection in a double-walled glass cylinder. One of the cylinder's two interior glass panels could be slid open to change the products on display with each new product release. On the wall, rough cemented excelsior board painted white contrasted with the smooth, transparent surface of the cylindrical showcase. Seen from above, in the second floor lounge where customers could design their own bespoke Air Force 1s, the showcase resembled an aquarium populated with a school of Air Force 1 "fish" swimming within the pool of a pelagic blue carpet that rippled out around it.

Straightforward

Nothing more, nothing less. Interiors designed in a straightforward manner celebrate space itself, making it easier to understand and easier to use. When it comes to retail and branded space, a forthright design presents product with clarity, candor, and a less strident sales pitch. Via lightly finished or even naked materials, clear forms, fewer (though still eloquent) color schemes, frankness makes the customer feel like an adult.

For those who appreciate unvarnished environments, gimmicks and clichés are just distracting, the are obstacles instead of enticements. These brand spaces are not pretending to be something they are not. In Italy, the **Goods** store embraces its nature as a place of commerce where shoppers have choices and deserve to understand what they are at a glance. To this end, the entire store is a vast, sophisticated display system that folds into its own shell, and nothing else. It leaves the rest of shopping to the shopper.

Sao Paulo's **Zeferino** boutique didn't have much to work with so it used what it had to its advantage. With only a 2.5-meter-wide site, the architect let the lot determine its look, turning a handicap into its asset. **Pascal Grasso** contended with constraints, as well. He had to turn two hallways into a Parisian fashion boutique. Using MDF blocks, he gave the corridors a sculpted look, but without ever trying to pretend they weren't interstitial space. Instead, he made a virtue of the fact that the store is a passage instead of a destination in order to draw shoppers into its depths.

Straight-up spaces appeal to those who do not necessarily want to star in their own feature film or run away to join the circus; those who long for an unmediated moment—no filters and no fantasies, just a one-to-one relationship between what they see and what they get.

T Magi
2009 / Hellerup, Denmark

WE ARCHITECTURE
Client: T Magi

While many shops tend to make a clear distinction between storefront and interior, the design of this tea shop allows the shop in Hellerup, Denmark itself to be perceived as its display window. WE turned to the teapot and the laboratory to create the visual scheme, the logo, and communications materials. A Scent Wall encourages shoppers to smell the 40 teas displayed, have a taste, read the WE-designed tea folder, and browse the Mariage Frères products on sale. Tiny backlit CNC-milled holes perforate the shelves and rear wall providing a large-scale, three-dimensional pattern that consolidates into the image of a teapot when viewed from afar, but dissipates as visitors approach, turning into the shop's minimalist furnishings, seemingly hewn from large swathes of white pegboard.

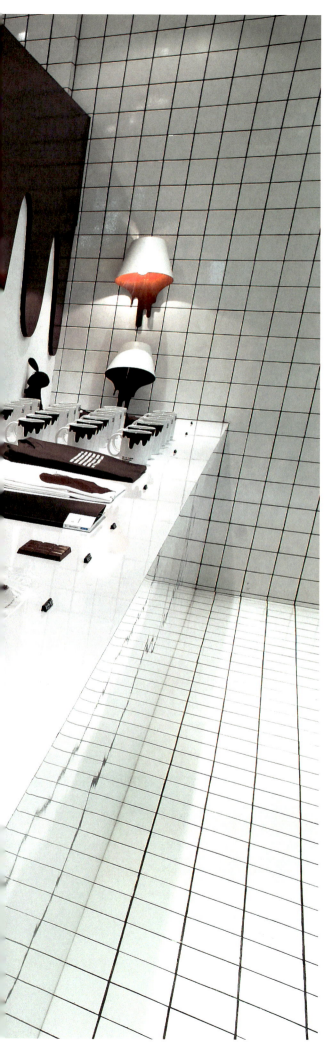

Chocolate Research Facility

2008 / Singapore

ASYLUM

Client: Chocolate Research Facility

Asylum's Singapore shop for CRF, the second, has the clinical look of a boutique laboratory. Its white laminate displays are set against a gridded backdrop of floor and walls clad in white glossy tiles that contrast with glossy brown polyurethane sprayed chocolate drips. The tiles are 100 x 100 mm which seems apt since the shop's claim to fame is its unprecedentedly broad product selection: chocolate bars in 100 flavors. The design started from the product packaging, which is a cross between pharmaceutical pill box and candy box, and continues through even the mold of the sweets themselves. Asylum also helped name the store: "a name that sounds very serious and a little too long, but appropriate," is what was required. In the chicly sterile Singapore outlet, playful elements like the overflowing chocolate wall and the slab tables draw in consumers of all ages as the content of the store is plainly visible from the kerb through the huge unframed windows that front the box-like interior.

Fifth Avenue Shoe Repair - Concept Store
2009 / Stockholm, Sweden

GUISE
Client: Fifth Avenue Shoe Repair

Local studio Guise designed a concept store in Stockholm for a Swedish fashion label that deconstructs traditional types of clothing to create unconventional, hybrid garments. Guise translated this approach into architecture by distorting various interior elements. The focal point of the black-and-white concept store is a helical stair made from black lacquered steel deformed into display surfaces and furnishings. Designers Jani Kristoffersen and Andreas Ferm wanted objects to feel ambiguous, resembling one thing while clearly serving another purpose. Wall shelves consist of a cubical steel-rod framework accompanied by hundreds of thin black steel plates that allow salespeople to rearrange the display by altering their composition.

Puramania
2009 / São Paulo, Brazil

GUILHERME TORRES

Client: Puramania

Despite an awkward, narrowing site, São Paulo-based Torres created a futuristic 354-square-meter boutique for a young Brazilian fashion brand. He embraced his handicap, making the narrowest point of the building the core of the store. Cubes, made from metal covered with epoxy-painted drywall, rise and fall throughout the space, sometimes hanging from the ceiling, other times emerging from the floor, or giving shape to counters, niches, showcases, and lighting fixtures. Torres composed the glossy furnishings in sci-fi geometric shapes, including an angular three-legged chair.

Corian Design Studio

2010 / Shanghai, China

MICHAEL YOUNG
Client: DuPont Corian

Hong Kong-based, British-born designer Michael Young designed the first Dupont Corian Design Studio in Asia. While demonstrating the range of the material's applications, the Shanghai showroom, like much of Young's work, also looks to bring eastern and western cultures together, uniting traditional Chinese art and building techniques with modern technology. Young set the space up to resemble a gallery, with generous doses of empty space. He also used the latest three-dimensional CNC technology, along with machinery purpose-built for the project, to create a curved wall featuring thousands of "bricks" that give the structure what appears oxymoronically to be a super-solid fluidity. Other vignettes include a high-speed train interior, along with contemporary bathrooms and kitchens.

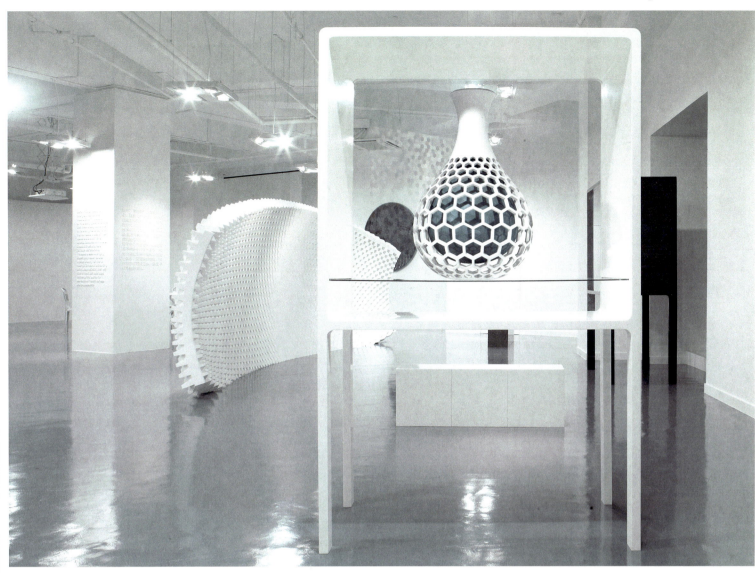

Stella K
Showroom
2011 / Paris, France

PASCAL GRASSO
Client: Stella K

For Parisian prêt-à-porter clothier
Stella K, Grasso used gray lacquered
MDF in random volumes protruding
from the walls to create a dynamic
office space and showroom on the
Champs Élysées. He had only two corridors, each more than 35 m long, to
create the shop but managed to turn
a constraint into a virtue. His highly
textural solution was surprisingly
straightforward: He transformed the
corridors into a display area and thereby the showroom itself. The dominant,
monolithic piece of furniture was made
of racks for storage of supplies and di-
vide the public retail space from private
offices and storage. Generating depth,
texture, and rhythm by extending the
display shelves into the halls, he turned
the passage into the destination.

Zeferino Jardins
2008 / São Paulo, Brazil

STUDIO ARTHUR CASAS
Client: Zeferino

Necessity was the mother of invention for the architects at Studio Arthur Casas: On São Paulo's Oscar Freire shopping boulevard, at two meters, the extremely narrow lot available to fashion label Zeferino ended up giving the store as much character as it denied it space. A wooden box with ramps and angled ceilings at the same inclination as the floor, it uses a mirror to give the illusion of a much larger interior.

[1]

[1] DOUBLE OO '96
[2] DOUBLE OO '09
2009 / Fukuoka, Japan

KOICHI FUTATSUMATA

Client: Alohanine Co., Ltd.
See also page 82

In Fukuoka, Japan, Futatsumata was tasked with turning a terrace shed on a gabled roof into a fashion retailer's office and showroom. Faced with a chaos of beams and pillars that had been improvised over the building's half century of existence, the designer reinforced everything and covered floors, walls, and garrets with gray flooring, to create a seamless interior where the clothes and the history of the room, itself, give the space its character. Futatsumata's second shop for fashion retailer Alohanine is defined by a pair of curves. One large curve expands obliquely into the interior, giving a view onto the street in front while the other, more gentle curve of the ceiling runs perpendicular to it.

[2]

DURAS Daiba
2009 / Tokyo, Japan

SINATO:
CHIKARA OHNO, MASAKI ITO

Client: Duras Inc.
See also page 88

Situated in a mall, Tokyo-based Sinato's Duras Daiba boutique for Duras eschewed the mall-bound look of its neighbors. The designers took advantage of a 3.65-meter-high ceiling by installing a drop ceiling made of expanded metal at 2.25 meter and setting up a stepped platform that leads shoppers to an "attic" space or mezzanine serving as a display for handbags, high heels, and mannequins. Shoppers choose their route through the space: the long way around at floor level or the shortcut for those willing to climb a bit.

Northern Lights
2006 / Amsterdam, Netherlands

BEARANDBUNNY
Client: Iittala
See also page 100

"Everyday life is yours to design," declares Finnish glass manufacturer Iittala. For the brand's Amsterdam shop, local designers John Maatman and Carlijn Kriekaard used the company's mix-and-match design philosophy as a springboard. The store's layout was desgned to allow customers to easily view, select, and combine pieces from the collection, while various elements celebrate the brand's history: The partitioned floor recreates that of the company's first factory, shingles on the wall recall those typically used to clad the faces of Finnish houses and steel slats criss-cross the storefront refering to patterns in an old Iittala architectural design by Alvar Aalto. The shop's centerpiece features drinking glasses in the company's remarkable color spectrum stacked in a composition that mimics the aurora borealis, or Northern Lights, for which Finland is also renowned.

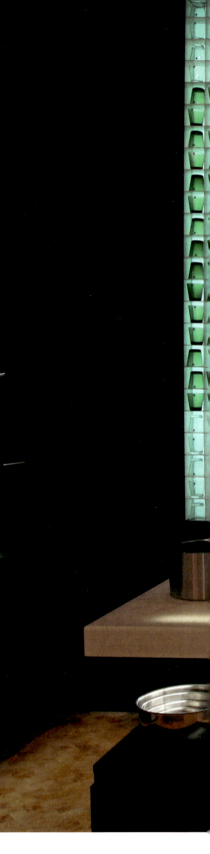

United Nude Flagship Store New York 1

2010 / New York, USA

REM D KOOLHAAS
Client: United Nude

United Nude is a women's shoe (and expanding fashion) brand founded by architect and creative director Rem D Koolhaas and seventh generation shoemaker Galahad Clark. From injection molded shoes to high-end carbon fiber heels, UN products have conceptual origins, highly structural forms, and an emphasis on innovation. Koolhaas' "dark shop" design for the New York flagship means that the store remains completely dark in areas other than those in which the products are showcased and, literally, highlighted. Two other features define the black space: The Wall of Light, a computer-controlled LED wall that displays footwear as works of art encapsulated in geometric frames like a high-end automat and a Lo Res car, a sculpture that does not provide seating and seems to have been carved out of obsidian as part of the brand's Lo Res fashion series.

ZUO Corp.
Pop-Up Shop
2009 / Warsaw, Poland
SUPER SUPER:
HANNA KOKCZYŃSKA,
JACEK MAJEWSKI,
AGNIESZKA
KUCZYŃSKA
Client: ZUO Group

In Warsaw, local design studios Super Super and Inside Outside let mirrors, LED light strips, and a meager budget define a four-month retail space for independent clothing brand Zuo Corp. Housed in a black box made from two interconnected, disused cargo containers placed in front of one of the city's most popular downtown cafes, its exterior gave no indication of its contents, The 27-square-meter interior was divided into a sales hall, storage area, and changing room. Walls and ceiling were tiled with mirrors, which, repeated ad infinitum by their own reflections, gave the illusion of a much deeper space. All interior seams were highlighted with LED strips, which provided the only (Tron-like) source of illumination in the room.

155

C. & E. Fein Brand-World Exhibition
2007 / Schwäbisch Gmünd, Germany

BÜROMÜNZING DESIGNER + ARCHITEKTEN
Client: C. & E. Fein GmbH

Looking to honor its illustrious predecessors, Fein, the company that invented the first portable drill and the first electrical tool ever, commissioned Stuttgart-based Büromünzing to make a brand presentation at the company's Schwäbisch Gmünd, Germany headquarters. In the foyer of their new expertise and development center, the resulting minimalist industrial exhibition showcased the company in a gorgeously straightforward way. The show included a two-story wall ornamented with drills, a wall of inventors, detailing the company's technical milestones, an interactive presentation that highlighted brand values, and three zones that illustrated the use of Fein products in the metal, construction, and automotive markets. Wisely, the designers opted to create an exhibition that let the product speak for itself—it proved to be an eloquent product.

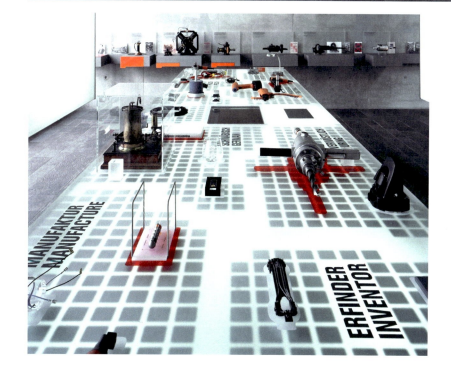

[1]

[2]

[1] FREITAG Flagship Store
2006 / Zurich, Switzerland

FREITAG LAB AG, SPILLMANN ECHSLE
Client: FREITAG

FREITAG Store
[2] *2009 / Berlin, Germany*
[3] *2002 / Hamburg, Germany*
[4] *2011 / Vienna, Austria*
[5] *2011 / New York, USA*

FREITAG LAB AG
Client: FREITAG

Since 1993, FREITAG bags—made from old truck tarpaulins—have been popular for their clean design, sustainable ethos, Swiss durability, and one-off character. So are their shops. In Hamburg, Blauraum architects cut apertures in freight containers and placed them end to end to create a long 140-square-meter room-within-a-room, or as the company has dubbed it, the "Mirrored Truckstop Shop," in the so far much-neglected Kreiz district. As much landmark as showroom, Spillmann Echsle stacked 17 colorful cargo containers to create the 120-square-meter, Zurich flagship tower, replete with a 25-meter-high observation platform. In Berlin, the shop racks "sprout out of the ground," borrowing a modular concept typical of Swiss gymnasiums.

[3]

[4]

[5]

Livraria da Vila
2007 / São Paulo, Brazil

ISAY WEINFELD
Client: Livraria da Vila

Facilitating the customer's easy, comfortable experience of the product—in this case, the book—drove São Paulo architect Isay Weinfeld's design of a local branch of the Livraria da Vila bookshop. Comfort took the form of cozy low-ceilinged spaces, dark tones, indirect lighting, and infinite shelves —in strategic disarray. Books are visible in all directions, their profusion reminiscent of a used book store, allowing shoppers to feel at ease browsing, leafing through or even reading on the couches and easy chairs dispersed at every level. The dramatic entrance—a vast, pivoting combination of window opening, bookshelf and doorway—suggests that a certain safe enchantment awaits guests within.

Palazzo delle Esposizioni Bookstore
2006 / Rome, Italy

OFFICINA DEL DISEGNO
Client: Palazzo delle Esposizioni

Rome's Palazzo delle Esposizioni art bookstore is part of a larger renovation project that is intended to integrate commercial space into the museum. The shop is dominated by a slightly twisted drop ceiling perforated with rectangular ribbon windows that seems, despite its monumental weight, to be billowing and swaying gently on a gust of wind.

Goods
Temporary Store
2011 / Brescia, Italy

ANTONIO GARDONI
Client: Ascom

Goods is the advent calendar of commercial space: Antonio Gardoni played with ordinary components and retail stereotypes to create an ever-shifting display system containing apertures, niches, shelving, drawers, and pockets that are folded into the walls. Though the shop's inventory hadn't been selected before the design phase, Gardoni built this temporary store for Ascom, in an outlet mall in Brescia, to sell anything and everything, from clothes and home décor to guitars and books, in a simultaneously remarkable and boilerplate way and on a rotating basis. The designer created an outwardly uniform, gunmetal gray floor-to-ceiling wall system, choosing a color that emphasizes products in the store while also emphasizing the store's presence amongst surrounding outlet shops. Gardoni threaded this interior wall, which extends 60 cm into the room, with door hinges, sliding guides, pivoting systems, counterweighted panels, accordion doors, roller blinds, and drawers, among other banal mechanical elements, in order to embed countless reconfigurable display opportunities in the architecture itself.

Vagabond Travel Bookshop
2008 / Stockholm, Sweden

SMÅNSK DESIGN STUDIO
Client: Vagabond Media

Viken, Sweden designers Martin Pålsson and Simon Jarl refreshed the look of the Stockholm bookshop run by the country's leading travel magazine *Vagabond*. In parallel with the company's tagline, "The whole world on your shelf," they designed the interior around notions of proximity, distance, and multidimensionality. A map is common to, and a symbol of, all types of travel and the patterns indicating streets on a map bear some passing resemblance to the forms required to build a bookshelf. This simple but elegant interpretation let Smånsk bring the city into the shop: A local area map provided the foundation for the skewed grid pattern on the floor, which then travels up the walls in the form of a graphical yellow shelving system. Segments corresponding to parks on the map were elevated off the floor, acting as merchandise display. On one wall, the words of Saint Augustine become a graphical device, like a map legend writ in text: "The world is a book, and those who do not travel read only a page."

[1]

[3]

[2]

MYKITA Shop

[1] *2009 / Vienna Austria*
[2] *2010 / Zurich,*
Switzerland
[3] *2010 / Tokyo, Japan*
[4] *2007 / Berlin, Germany*
[5] *2011 / Berlin, Germany*

MYKITA TEAM

Client: Mykita GmbH

Designed by German eyewear upstart MYKITA's four founders, the company's signature shop walls are assembled from countless Dexion corner plates, typically used as supporting brackets for heavy-load modular shelving. Their L-shaped cross-sections, dotted with a series of holes, enable a variety of shelf-mounting configurations. Powder-coated with a lustrous white finish, they are arranged side by side in all the shops to form back-lit, light-permeable walls. The huge flexibility of the Dexion system has also formed the basis for MYKITA store shelves, desks/ work stations, and countless other retail elements that must be sturdy, quick to build, and cost-effective. Also common to all the shops, obsolete Swissair mobile flight attendant trolleys serve as sales and display surfaces. Unique to the original MYKITA Shop in Berlin, an interactive neon-light installation generates a pulsing animation sequence over the walls during business hours. Once the shop closes, however, sensors installed on the facade detect movement along the kerb, allowing the light to "follow" passersby who often stop for a minute to interact with the light. In the evening, this light show is only emphasized by the subdued street lighting around it. The Mykita Shop Zurich features an open-plan design with the Dexion display wall following the curved façade of its 1930s-era building. In the 18m2 Vienna shop a series of mirrors increases the room's apparent size while enabling customers to view themselves from a range of angles when trying on glasses. Although Mykita Tokyo is located in the basement of a narrow building, it's large storefront floods it with light during the day and showcases the bright white interior at night. To tide customers over until the original Berlin store can be renovated, this two-month, 32-square-meter, €7.000 pop-up borrows space inside the fashion store Apartment.

[4]

[5]

Open Lounge
2011 / Zurich, Switzerland

NAU
Client: Raiffeisen Schweiz

Raiffeisen Schweiz's flagship branch on Zurich's Kreuzplatz reconsiders the role of the contemporary bank by dissolving the traditional barriers between customer and employee. Today, technology makes banking infrastructure largely invisible: employees access terminals concealed in furnishings, while a robotic retrieval system grants round-the-clock access to safety deposit boxes secured in the vault. This frees the public space to become a bright-white, light-filled environment, completely transparent to the street (which cannot help but be symbolic in this day and age). Here, customers can learn about new services and products, and conversations can start spontaneously around a touchscreen-equipped information table and then transition to meeting rooms for more private discussions. Ribbon-like high-pressure laminate walls, digitally milled with abstract portraits of the neighborhood's prominent former residents, carefully filter views through the interiors to create varying degrees of privacy and maximizing the penetration of natural light throughout. This studied decoration anchors the business in the area's cultural past, while moving it clearly into the future.

[1]

The Deutsche Bank BrandSpace

2011 / Frankfurt, Germany

ART+COM, COORDINATION

Client: Deutsche Bank AG

In the modernized Deutsche Bank headquarters in Frankfurt / Main, Art+Com and Coordination sculpted the BrandSpace to highlight the bank's history and philosophy, transforming the company's iconic logo created by Anton Stankowski in the 1970s into a three-dimensional space. The Brand-Space is the continuation of the three-dimensional Logo Concept begun in 2005 in communication and carried on in 2009 via the new Corporate Design. Using the principles of anamorphosis, they turned it into a series of abstract three-dimensional logo "sculptures" that must be viewed from a specific vantage point to be recognizable. In the first [1] installation, the guilloché moves over the surface of a sensitive multi-touch surface, morphing into letters and thus becoming the point of entry into a space providing information about the company. In the second [2], reactive installation, flowing guilloché patterns are projected onto the back wall. Visitors entering the space are detected by a three-dimensional tracking device and their shapes appear in the projection as a series of lines tracing their silhouette. As the visitors move, they trigger a display of statistical information.

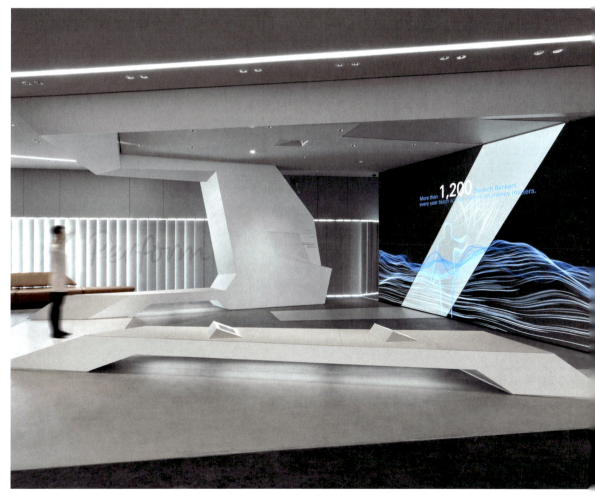

[2]

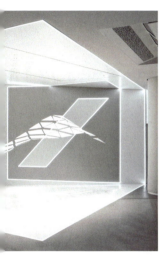

In the third installation [3], the logo becomes a kinetic sculpture with the central, diagonal element sliced into 48 moving triangles mapped with video images. The last [4] element consists of a faceted mirror and projected blue light. Visitors initially see only the mirror and dynamic blue reflections, but as they approach, a single image begins to consolidate before their eyes, ultimately resolving itself into the bank logo. This moment encapsulates the brand attitude, placing people front and center in relation to the company: It is only through the visitor's movement toward the mirror that the brand logo can assume its form. The customer creates the bank.

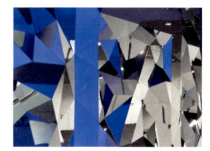

[4]

Bastard Bowl
2008 / Milan, Italy

STUDIO METRICO
Client: Comvert s.r.l., Bastard Milanese

Studiometrico designed the local offices, design studio, flagship store, and storage facility for skate and snowboard fashion brand Comvert's Bastard label—complete with a skate bowl. Following extensive research into employee habits, Bini and Murialdo began to refurbish a 1400-square-meter 1940s cinema with the goal of creating a space that would cultivate and sustain constant communication amongst Bastard teams. The cinema's 70-square-meter main entrance became the first Bastard store, conceived not only as retail, but as a community-building space, where Comvert collaborators and employees will work a shift each month to stay in close contact with the product they design and the people to whom they distribute and sell it. The designers preserved existing elements, including grand stairs and marble floors, supplementing them with waste wood panels and off-cuts generated throughout the project. Suspended six meters over the products depot, the 200-square-meter skate bowl maintains a visual and spatial relationship with the design department. Built from glue-laminated wood and curved steel beams, it was designed by the four skaters who founded Comvert.

GOING PUBLIC

Actual brandscapes—outdoor, public spaces—usually have to contend with crowded, chaotic, or sensory-saturating surroundings, or just find a way to work with, instead of being trumped by, Mother Nature. Not surprising then, that these projects tend to tap more of our senses than just our vision.

Bompas & Parr's Ziggurat of Fruit had to compete for the attention of spectators at an outdoor music festival. Their Ziggurat, where concert-goers inhaled fruit, absorbing its nutrients through their lungs and eyeballs, was a Willy Wonkan adventure complete with a vertical labyrinth. It was not just a theatrical piece of architecture; it was a recreational experience that could not be repeated.

To celebrate seating as an historical design object as much as a piece of office equipment, **Design hoch Drei** (d3) collaborated with the verdant German countryside through which they built a temporary footpath. They dotted the trail with improvised and highly irregular benches, stools, and armchairs and, instead of trying to outdo the outdoors, d3 used the landscape to frame the furniture with great subtlety. The result was a surreal scenography that forced hikers to look at both seating and scenery anew.

In Seoul, **Mass Studies** brought the outdoors entirely indoors with its design of the **Ann Demeulemeester Shop**. The shop is wallpapered with lush hanging gardens (almost a textile in their own right) and an unobtrusive irrigation system that waters them with mist. Shoppers browse in a rainforest imbued with an earthy aroma, engaging a sense to which architecture is all too often indifferent.

When passerby finally notice **Electrolux**'s nomadic restaurants, **The Cube** and **Nomiya**, perched atop local landmarks like, say, Brussels' Parc du Cinquantenaire or Paris' Palais de Tokyo, they rarely remain indifferent. These boxes need only to be craned into place on firm soil, a solid roof or a tranquil body of water to open for business. They have the lightweight flexibility of an exhibition stand since they travel around Europe, but the complex design of permanent architecture. Symbiotic architecture, they borrow a little real estate for a little while, while endowing the public spaces they colonize with a sense of discovery, an unexpected prosthetic beauty, and an ethos of luxury. In part, it is the luxury of having a once-in-a-lifetime experience.

Rapha Mobile Cycle Club

2011 / Various locations in Europe

WILSON BROTHERS
Client: Rapha
<u>See also page 64</u>

For bicyclist clothing and accessories label, Rapha, the London-based Wilson Brothers converted a caravan into the Rapha Mobile Cycle Club, a combination gallery, shop, café, and community-building space. The 7.5-ton Club drove from event to event across Europe weekly, changing its look and content at each stop. The brothers enabled this by equipping the vehicle with an exterior display system, comprising a grid of ring-hooks affixed to the flank of the vehicle, and a retractable awning, beneath which a set of six glazed-top oak-and-steel display tables showcased Rapha product, publications, and ephemera while doubling as picnic tables from which to view race footage whilst enjoying a coffee.

Interstuhl Pfad

*2011 / Meßstetten-
Tieringen, Germany*

DESIGN HOCH DREI

Client: Interstuhl Büromöbel GmbH
& Co. KG

The Interstuhl Trail was designed
by Design Hoch Drei (d3) as a voyage
of discovery through the exquisite
Tieringen countryside in Germany
to educate viewers about the wide
variety of seating that exists. Along
the path, hikers experienced alternating moments of movement and rest,
excitement and relaxation, on a series
of unusual seats. Made by local crafts-
men and international architects, these
seats, like sculptural signposts, were
positioned at the most beautiful vista
points and echoed the formal language
of the Interstuhl Arena, a brand space
that was also designed by d3. D3 also
contributed signage consisting of
simple concrete blocks with recessed
numbers and screenprinted information. These helped hikers find their way
without disturbing the environment
or competing visually with the seating
pieces themselves.

Kuh-Watching

2009 / Berlin, Germany

**BÜRO FÜR
GESTALTUNG:**
JOHANNA RICHTER,
ROBERT HASLBECK,
DAVID
OELSCHLÄGEL,
JOHANNES ALBERT

Sponsor: Hornbach

See also page 186

During this self-initiated project, supported by German DIY franchise Hornbach, the Berlin-based designers looked to timber beams and boards, straw, milk and hay for their materials. In just three days, they built a temporary paddock for real cows in a gap between buildings in Prenzlauer Berg, in the middle of Berlin, to underscore the modern consumer's increasing estrangement from agricultural life by creating a contrast between urban and rural idylls. The 3,500 visitors received free milk available in the flavours chocolate, elder, and almond and when the installation was taken down, all of the building materials were re-used to build the designers' offices.

Yukon Bay

2010 / Hanover, Germany

DAN PEARLMAN

Client: Zoo Hannover GmbH

Yukon Bay is a themed world recreating the landscape and pioneer spirit of Canada at Hanover's Adventure Zoo. The 22,000-square-meter park took Berlin experience-architects at Dan Pearlman nine years to develop. In the process, they moved 15,000 cubic meters of earth, used 1,200 tons of steel and 13,000 cubic meters of concrete, 200 tons of natural stone, 39 panes of specialty glass for dioramas on land and underwater, and landscaped 200 copses with 18,000 shrubs and perennials. Outside of ice hockey, Yukon Bay may be Canada's finest marketing effort—and most striking brandscape—to date.

Ziggurat of Flavour

2010 / Ledbury, UK

BOMPAS & PARR
Client: Big Chill, Fairtrade Fruit
See also page 226

For the one-week Big Chill music festival in Ledbury, the 40-ton steel Ziggurat of Flavour was a pyramidal art installation designed by home-grown food architects Bompas & Parr, containing a cloud of breathable fruit where visitors supplemented their recommended daily dietary allowances by inhaling. After navigating through optical illusions and a three-story labyrinth of vaporized Fairtrade fruit inside, visitors emerged—healthier—onto a grand slide at the pinnacle. Ziggurat was inspired by 18th-century Cuccagna monuments, vast architectural structures constructed from food and based on the tale of the Land of Cockaigne, a mythical Eden built on mountains of cheese, watered by pastry rainstorms, and where all game was already cooked and waiting to be eaten. As in the past, Bompas & Parr consulted with space scientists to ensure that the fruits' nutrients would be absorbed through vistors' lungs and eyeballs.

[1] Boombox
2009 / London, UK

[2] Giant Knitting
2010 / Nationwide, UK

STUDIO XAG
Client: Diesel
See also pages 47 and 98

For the brand's eight-week promotion of its new Diesel U Music Radio, London's XAG designed, built, and installed three wooden boomboxes, totalling 30 meters in length, as if they were second skins lining the Diesel Carnaby Street storefront.
In 11 store windows around the UK, XAG used jersey, wadding, cardboard, wool, and plywood to create vastly oversized sculptural objects related to knitting and the sartorial trades. The goal was to promote and present Diesel's Fall/Winter 2010 knitwear collection in a fresh, visually arresting fashion.

[1]

Glücksfabrik

2010 / Erbach, Germany

TINO VALENTINITSCH

Client: Koziol Glücksfabrik

The Koziol Luck Factory in Erbach, Germany focuses on good fortune and the creation of a better life. Stephan Koziol, son of the founder Bernhard Koziol, commissioned a space showing the history and current story of the company in a scenographic and playful way. Designed by New York-based Tino Valentinitsch (although the store, Glückstor, is the work of Milan-based Maria Christina Hamel), it generates multimedia experiences of the brand via fantastical "machinery" such as the Time Cone, Peace Machine, and Design Generator. It is a space that offers pop cultural entertainment, information, and a positive, if unusual, experience of the brand.

Love Sweets Antique Aoyama
2010 / Tokyo, Japan

GLAMOROUS:
YASUMICHI MORITA
Client: Club Antique Co., Ltd.
See also page 254

This enchanted 17-square-meter Tokyo shop specializes in sweets that are both candy and eye candy. Club Antique's primary product, the colorful glazed Toronama doughnut, which was imagined as a confection for a forest fairy with a serious sweet tooth, was used as the starting point for the design of everything from chandeliers and candelabras to signage and images frosting the facade.

Smart Urban Stage
2010 / Berlin, Germany

BRAUNWAGNER
Client: Daimler AG

For a 10-week event hosted by auto-maker Daimler in Berlin, Aachen-based Braunwagner erected a stage that served as a temporary communication platform where topics such as electric mobility, sustainability, and innovative ideas for urban living were presented to the public. The lightweight inflatable membrane, tear-resistant and scal-able from 250 to 380 square meter, it was designed to fit into diverse spaces across Europe. The stage was inspired, both formally and functionally, by the tridion cell, the stiff snub-nosed struc-tural shell of a smart car designed to avoid injury and heavy damage during a collision. Cost-efficient and eco-friendly, the membrane can be shipped easily and inexpensively, assembled and taken down quickly while still fea-turing state-of-the-art, energy-saving media technology.

Nomiya / Palais de Tokyo
2009 / Paris, France

ART HOME
Client: Electrolux, Palais de Tokyo

Artist Laurent Grasso and his brother, the architect Pascal Grasso modeled this prosthetic restaurant on the interiors of certain Japanese bars and cinematographic techniques. Nomiya or Art Home is a collaboration between home appliance manufacturer Electrolux and the cultural institution on whose roof it was perched, Palais de Tokyo. A perforated screen wrapping the glass and steel container suggested an aurora borealis. Thanks to its porosity, the 12-guest chef's table enjoyed a remarkable view over Paris, as well as into chef Gilles Stassart's kitchen.

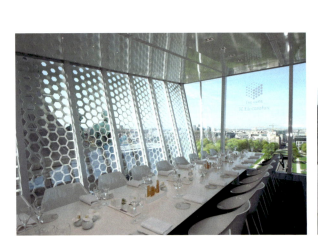

The Cube
by Electrolux
2011 / Various locations

PARK ASSOCIATI
Client: Electrolux Appliance Spa

A symbiotic piece of architecture, Electrolux's itinerant restaurant, The Cube, can be craned temporarily into any unexpected or striking location. Designed by the Milanese firm Park Associati and built from glass, aluminium, Corian, and wood, the pavilion opened in Brussels, perched for three months atop the Parc du Cinquantenaire, close to the headquarters of the European Community. Accommodating 18 diners per sitting, the filigreed structure will continue on to the roofs of buildings, monuments, and even waterways of Italy, Russia, Switzerland, and Sweden. Wrapped in an aluminium skin lasercut in a geometric pattern, the 140-square-meter interior is an open-plan space with an Electrolux-equipped kitchen, a 50-square-meter terrace, and a single large table that can be raised into the ceiling to free up a lounge area for use after meals. The assemblage has the lightness and versatility of an exhibition booth but with the design complexity of a building—a high-tech, sustainable, and energy-saving building, at that.

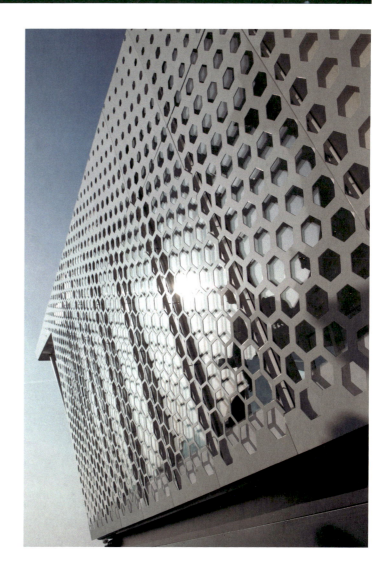

Ann Demeulemeester Shop

2010 / Seoul, South Korea

MASS STUDIES:
MINSUK CHO, KISU PARK, ZONGXOO U, BUMHYUN CHUN, JOONHEE LEE, JIEUN LEE, WON-BANG KIM

Client: Handsome Corp

Almost a city park in itself, the Ann Demeulemeester shop in Seoul contains both an allusion to the fashion designer's original Antwerp retail space and a careful adjustment to its densely urban site. The architects bubbled (outwards), radiused (the corners), and arched the new shop's storefront windows and skylights, which led, in turn, to the creation of a naturally swagging ceiling inside. Adjacent to a wooded park, the building was conceived as a sponge that absorbs the outside and draws it in. Stunning tiles sown with greenery dress the facade, roof, and interior basement walls. An irrigation system waters the tiles regularly, according to season, via a pipe passing through the top of each. The green walls diminish the building's energy use by cooling it. The basement, watered by a subtle mist system, becomes especially atmospheric, allowing city-locked visitors to shop in a rainforest amidst a nearly palpable earthy aroma, engaging a sense that architecture typically neglects.

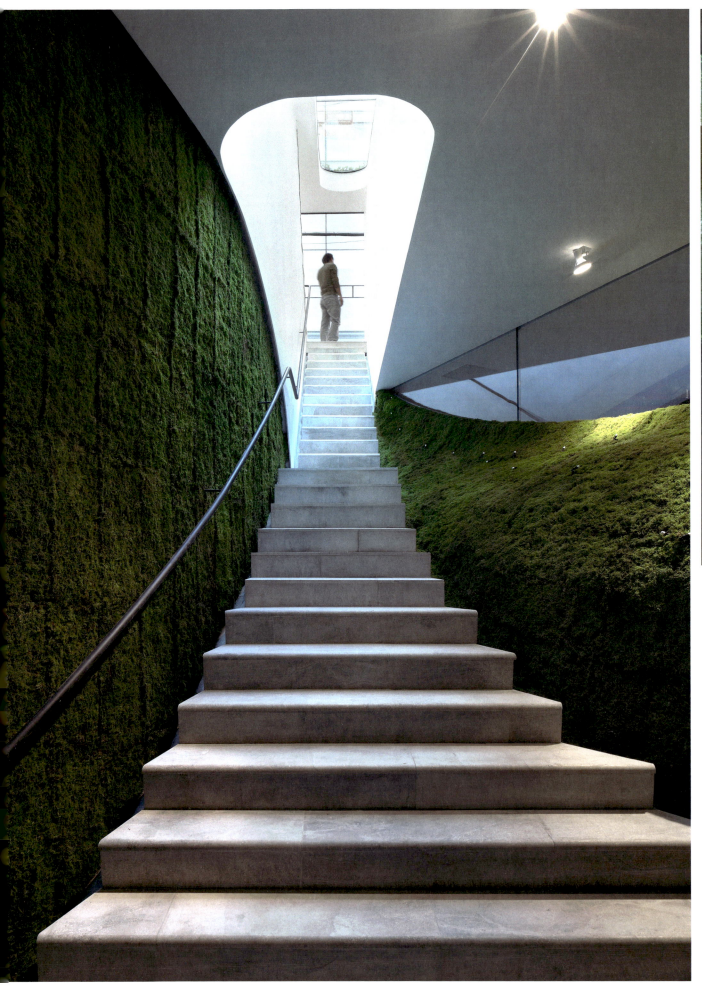

Garoa Store
2008 / São Paulo, Brazil

UNA ARQUITETOS
Client: Garoa

The Garoa store is located on a small corner lot on São Paulo's Oscar Freire shopping boulevard. Local architects UNA removed a slice of the building's volume, revealing the retail interior beyond two vast, perpendicular windows on the facade. Because the glazing does not run parallel to the street, this heightens the drama of the shop's relationship to the street. Rendered in black concrete, which resembles a charred stone and is cut at oblique angles, the architecture's overall effect is a sculptural one that amplifies the bright white interior and the merchandise within.

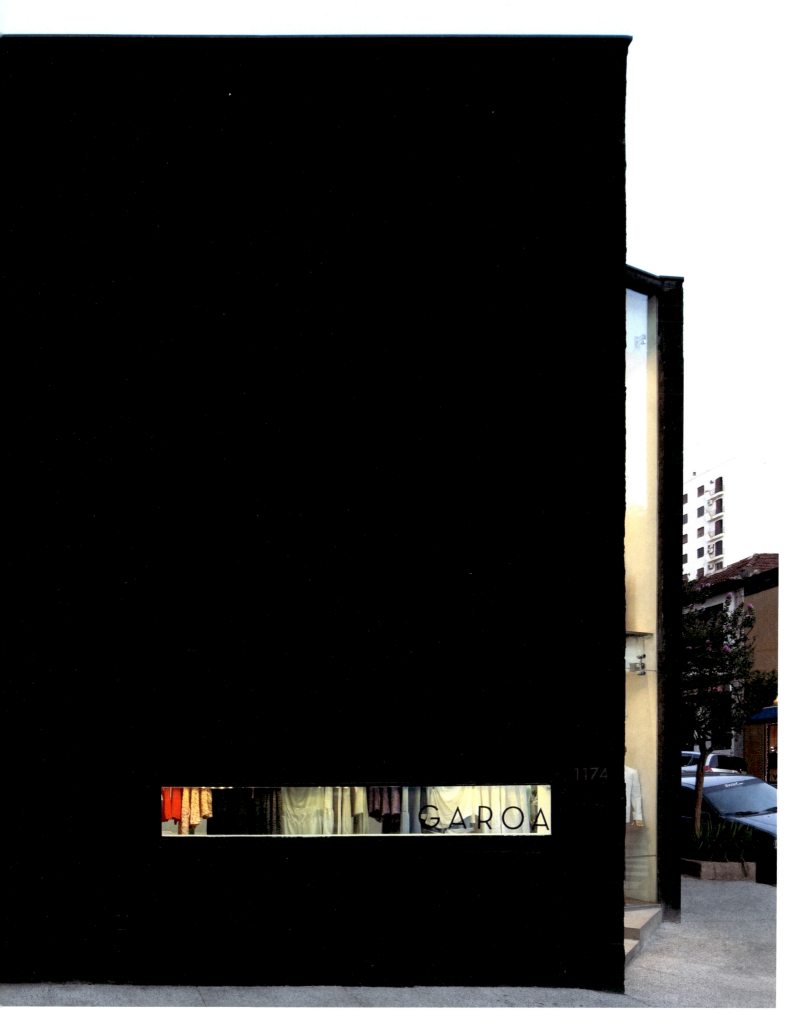

Soft Brutalism - Siki Im Concept Store
2010 / New York, USA

LEONG LEONG ARCHITECTS
Client: Siki Im

Manhattan-based architects Leong Leong filled an existing cargo container with a large ramp to create a temporary retail installation and gathering space for fashion designer Siki Im during the local Building Fashion event. They covered the ramp with soy-based spray foam leaving a soft gloppy surface into which they carved small niches and ledges to create areas for display and seating. Some of the structure was CNC-milled as a kit of parts; the whole thing was built off-site then dismantled and re-installed in the container in three days. Unusually for a boutique, the garments were hung out of sight in a low-slung cave hollowed out beneath the ramp and accessed through canted triangular portals on either end, encouraging visitors to explore the space for curiosity's sake alone and then discover the clothes in a wholly intimate environment.

Gerngross
2010 / Vienna, Austria

LOVE ARCHITECTURE AND URBANISM
Client: Deka Immobilien Investment GmbH

For Deka Immobilien Investment, Graz-based LOVE refurbished the 52,500-square-meter Gerngross store in Vienna while only minimally disrupting shoppers. To give the building a new axis, the architects focused on the atrium with its escalators, rounding and rolling the ceilings of the individual levels upwards, thereby seemingly enlarging and opening the space. This allows it to dovetail with retail areas and gives the building a seamless continuity. The retail areas are distributed like ice floes over each level, marked by a change in floor covering and ceiling material which forms a star-shaped pattern of paths on both the ceiling and floor, facilitating orientation within the building. The facade, where the ice floe theme continues the interior scheme, consists of large-scale, amorphous color fields, illuminated strategically in the evenings, that lie beneath an ornamental, semi-transparent screen that ensures a continuous view from the building into the street and doubles as a sun screen. A huge, amorphous, white-framed glazing gives the caged facade an intriguing asymmetry. Advertising media, such as logos and slide-in plates, were aggregated and drastically reduced. Depending on where passersby stand, they perceive the facade differently: From a level viewing angle, it looks like a white ornamental field. As the viewing angle gets steeper, the background color comes into focus, creating what the designers call a "tilting" effect.

Audi A8
Dealer Meeting
Barcelona 2010
2010 / Barcelona, Spain

SCHMIDHUBER +
PARTNER
ARCHITEKTUR
Client: Audi AG
See also page 216

As a branding effort, the Audio A8 dealers and importers launch was about more than logos and boasting. Munich-based Schmidhuber turned the area around Barcelona's Raventós winery into an Audi "brandscape." Using the tagline "The Art of Progress," the architects designed a two-day, six-location architecture—incorporating a low-slung building, furniture, and an entire "branded" valley—in which to present an emotional and subtle staging of the Audi A8 automobile. A silver beam-shaped building housing the A8 laboratories, partially sheathed in a white ribbon, represented a translation of the dynamics of the nearby race track into architectural language: the white wing of the lab structure continued the ribbon's arcing line before seemingly lifting off into the sky. The interior resembled an elongated wind tunnel, in which a profusion of mirrors gave the illusion of a much greater space. Here, the shape of the car's new single-frame grill with folded corners formed the central design element.

AreA1 2010
2010 / Barcelona, Spain

SCHMIDHUBER + PARTNER ARCHITEKTUR
Client: Audi AG
See also page 214

Roadshow AreA1 was envisioned as a mobile and modular architecture in which to introduce the A1 automobile to Europe. Starting on the pier in Barcelona, the Munich-based architectural team translated the message of the new design— young, urban, and high quality—into a detailed spatial experience. The radiused building modules, designed in kits ranging from 65 to 1,000-square-meter, took their shapes from the A1's single-frame radiator grille and could be arranged in multiple configurations depending on the city and setting. The abstract structures were anchored by ten-meter-wide and eight-meter high "A1" letters, were presented on a 25 x 34 meter wide, elevated stage, and hosted a lab, workshop, playground, and gallery filled with work by local artists. The Driving Experience was an extreme obstacle course that included a centrifugal test with 180-degree turns and a track through a quarter pipe. Demonstrating how every element of the design was intended to communicate the brand independently of the logos and marketing speak, specially designed programmable light poles with integrated sound systems created a swank, youthful atmosphere at night in the central A1 Marketplace, a popular outdoor meeting space complete with a bar, seating, lounge, and wireless local area network where AreA1 hosted concerts, nightclubs, and parties.

Glamor & Drama

Scenographic spaces choreograph experiences that are out of the ordinary. They replicate places we've never been or can never be, historical settings lost to time, gentlemen's clubs sacrificed to changing mores, and fairytale castles that few people believe in anymore.

They ask us to leave our mundane lives on the kerb for a few minutes and become either spectators or actors on a stage where the script of commerce is being played.

H&M's Home Reflections showroom took on a through-the-lookingglass quality. Surreal scenes in which clusters of cushions and chaises longues were suspended in columns between ceiling and floor mirrors lent secret life to seemingly unremarkable home furnishings.

Denis Košutić's series of Amicis boutiques lets shoppers escape into posh and lofty worlds. In one, an eclectic smattering of patrician objects, old and new, bestows highly stylized rooms with detailed character. In another, a baroque confusion of floral patterns and color invites shoppers into a lifesize dollhouse. A much larger dollhouse was built to broadcast the **Barbie** brand, whose Shanghai emporium embodies a powerful powder puff pink version of Glamor.

There are more fantastical experiences, as well: The abstracted underwater world of **Monki Sea of Scallops** by **Electric Dreams** includes jellyfish and wheeled seahorse displays. The submarine theme plucks shoppers out of their daily rounds and submerges them in a realm where shopping is a game, the interior is full of toys, and they have escaped time altogether.

The traveling **Lunar Pop-Up** by **///byn** went even further, helping visitors to escape gravity itself. The exhibition space and shop mimicked the meager volume of a lunar capsule. As visitors pass through geometric interior modules, Cartesian coordinates fall away, the orthogonal world bursts into shards, and an alien landscape sharpens into crystalline focus.

By allowing customers to escape outward, these spaces suggest that the brand and its products can help us to do the same inwardly if we take them home. The purchase is only a souvenir of the experience, the fragment of an emotion manifest. They offer a little commerce and a little catharsis.

Amicis Men Fashion Concept Store

2010 / Vienna, Austria

DENIS KOŠUTIĆ

Client: Amicis
See also pages 55 and 224

Georges Braque was a taxidermist, as Vienna-based designer Košutić points out. In the local Amicis men's shop, he pairs cubism with the sober architecture of the 1990s. Košutić coats every wall surface with multiple shades of brown, gray and black and alternatively draws the background or the foreground into focus. His version of interior flair comes in the form of wallpapers printed with quotations from Oscar Wilde's novel *The Picture of Dorian Gray*, taxidermied animals, and Persian carpets, evoking melancholy and nostalgia. The theatrical Blue Lounge suggests an interplay of dream and reality, the authentic and the artificial, earnestness and irony, which the designer associates with Dadaism. The elements, materials, and colors in this room — vintage furniture and luminaires, glossy synthetic surfaces, wood veneers, bold blue hues, and bizarre antique artifacts — can also be found scattered subtly across other areas of the shop, providing a sense of stylistic and therefore temporal restlessness.

Amicis Bel Etage Fashion Concept Store

2010 / Vienna, Austria

DENIS KOŠUTIĆ

Client: Amicis
See also pages 55 and 220

Vienna-based Košutić dovetailed real and surreal, classical and contemporary elements to create a palace of fashion in a long narrow interior. Košutić converted antique pieces of furniture to unexpected uses and re-interpreted and exaggerated various epochs of style through exuberant pairings of fabrics, wallpapers, stucco, wall claddings, and photo collages. By using countless nuanced shades of beige and brown, he gave the interior a subtle but dynamic monochrome appearance. Košutić calls this the "new restraint" and plays, in a high-handed way, with function. The clashing variety of cherrypicked materials, patterns, and ornaments gives surfaces an exuberant three-dimensionality. Clean-lined and unpatterned modern elements that pepper the space only serve to underscore the surrounding cacophony of shapes and styles.

Architectural
Punch Bowl
2009 / London, UK

BOMPAS & PARR
Client: Courvoisier
See also page 190

In 1694, they say, Admiral Edward
Russell filled a punchbowl so vast that
it onvolved 2,500 lemons and was
served by a small boy in a boat. For
Courvoisier, London-based architects
of the senses, Bompas & Parr "exploded"
the esteemed beverage to an even larger
scale. After six month's of research, for
a single week, the designers flooded 33
Portland Place with over four tons of
punch, enough for 25,000 giddy people.
The resulting punchbowl was so large
that international engineering firm
Arup was called in to ensure that the
building wouldn't collapse under the
weight of the alcohol. Visitors rowed
over the beverage before enjoying a
glassful while toying with the remote
control garnishes.

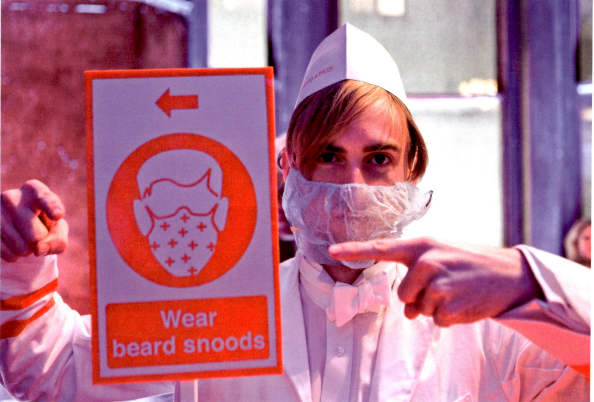

H&M Home Reflections Showroom

2009 / Stockholm, Sweden

UXUS

Client: H&M Hennes & Mauritz AB (H&M)

See also pages 60 and 241

Reversing current trends, UXUS' Stockholm showroom for the H&M Home Collection, a housewares line, transforms what was originally Hennes & Mauritz' virtual store into a bricks-and-mortar retail environment. In collaboration with the H&M design team, UXUS built mirrors above which they suspended clustered vignettes of furniture to create a "gallery" of fashionable products for the home. The installation imagined a world inside, if not through, the looking glass, in order to explore consumers' sometimes fraught, sometimes gratifying relationship with both identity and style.

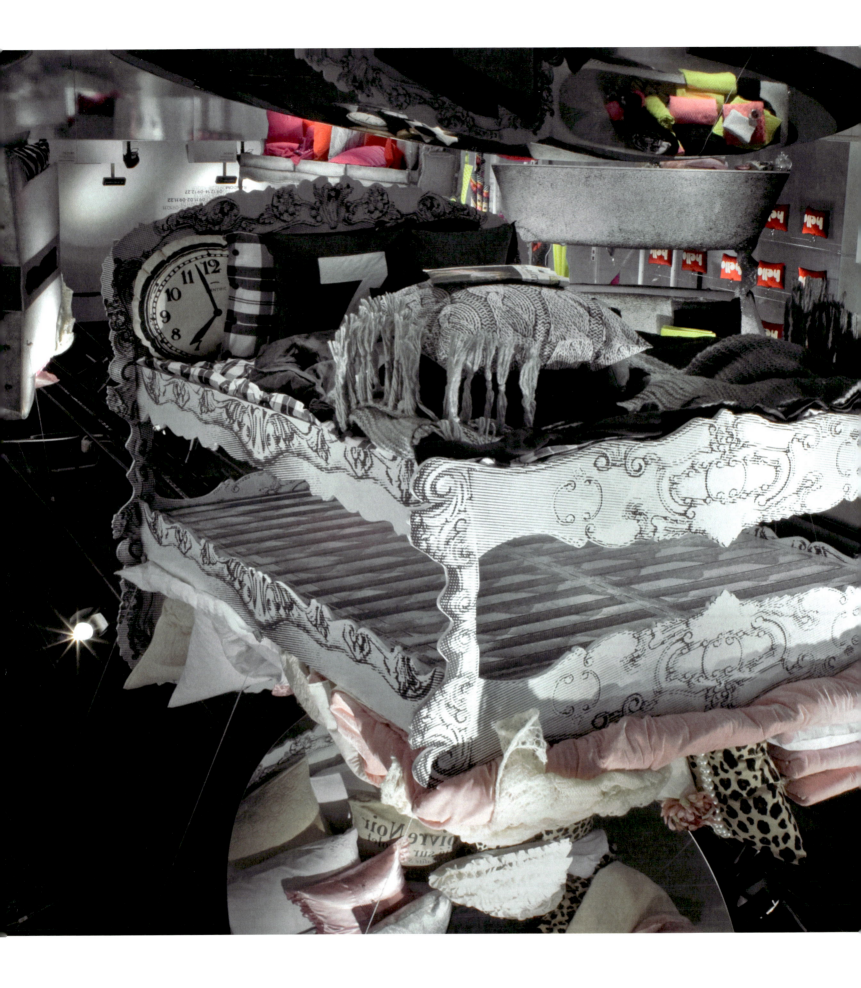

Roen
2006, 2007 /
Tokyo, Japan

ITO MASARU
Client: ROEN Co., Ltd.

To enter the Tokyo Roen boutique opened in 2006, customers press an intercom button and pass through a tunnel lined with black parachute fabric. Inside, the local designers divided a 95-square-meter interior into three discreetly themed spaces. The first minimalist space features mortar, glass, and steel and dramatic dimmable lighting. Passing through a second tunnel, visitors come upon a gallery paved with natural sand and finally a members' room accessible to only select clientele that is filled with antique furniture and old books. When open, a heavy iron door at the rear of the shop bathes the interior in natural light and reveals the image of an idyllic green river.

A year later, the firm created another location divided into three zones bisected obliquely with a black glass tunnel that dictates circulation. A custom-made Swarovski chandelier and a titanium skull cascade towards the floor while an antechamber to the fitting room is tiled in a colored leopard skin pattern and threaded with digital LEDs. The result? An eclectic mix of minimalism and opulence.

2006

2007

Aesop

[1] *2008 / Adelaide,*
Australia
[2] *2009 / Singapore*

MARCH STUDIO
Client: Aesop
See also page 108

Australian beauty brand Aesop's third store is an homage to the flourishing product market. March Studio constructed its entire ceiling system in Melbourne from 7,560 medicine bottles suspended from threaded rods, mounted to portable MDF panels and fixed to HySpan Beams, then disassembled and trucked it to Adelaide. Once emptied, the company's particle board packaging became the 41-square-meter store itself, forming display, storage units, and a service counter.

From cardboard boxes to amber glass bottles, Swiss hoarding boards to white porcelain, March Studio's multiple Aesop shop interiors represent an exploration into the opportunities and constraints entailed by the use of a local material. Their so-called "Stringapore" store responded to Singapore's unique struggle to find an identity beyond that imposed on it by the city's ubiquitous shopping malls and neon lights. Throughout history, Singapore has been a busy dot on the international trade route, a place passed through on the way to somewhere else. String represents this concept poetically, so March used 30 kilometers of coconut husk string, a regional product, to create an all-enveloping "chandelier." Brought together, the seemingly insignificant individual threads give the space a single powerful identity, making it a destination instead of merely a stop along the way.

[1]

[2]

GRACE Fashion House
2010 / Munich, Germany

HEIKAUS
Client: Sarah & Klaus Hallhuber

A Munich boutique for the Grace Fashion House, Heikaus, based in Mundelshelm, Germany, is defined by large faceted metallic plinths that descend from the ceiling and rise from the floor to frame vitrines holding accessories. Nearby, glass, polished stainless steel, and bronzed mirror-clad display tables echo the form of the angular drop ceiling above. The designers paired these crystalline, sculptural elements with tufted furnishings, radiused corners, plush carpet, and soft (though, again, metallic) drapery to strike a balance through contrasts.

The Art of Progress
2009 / Miami, USA

MUTABOR DESIGN
Client: Audi
See also page 36

Audi chose Art Basel / Design Miami, a show allying art and design, to introduce the Audi A8 to the US as a masterpiece of design and engineering, as well as the "highest art" of the automobile. Mutabor erected a Brobdingnagian stage furnished with a sofa, sideboard, and lounge lamp that dwarfed visitors to the booth as well as an actual A8, which at this scale looked like a model car, and therefore a design icon, ornamenting the coffee table. For fair attendees interested in modern avant-garde design and collectible cultural artifacts, the multidisciplinary Hamburg-based creative agency staged the car's debut in a narrative way that introduced the A8 as a piece of collectible culture itself and Audi, not merely as a logo-bound sponsor, but as an innovator on the international design scene.

Skins 6/2 Cosmetics
2010 / Las Vegas, USA

UXUS

Client: Supergaaf LLC
See also pages 60 and 230

Dutch cosmetics retailer SKINS 6|2 commissioned UXUS to create the brand's first pilot store in the US. Located at the Cosmopolitan Hotel in gaudy Las Vegas, the 200-square-meter interior juxtaposes simple elements in unusual ways. UXUS played with the scale of the space and, inspired by the dynamic nature of street markets, arranged loose groupings and stacks of products and familiar fixtures to make the shop feel accessible. They also included playful elements, like the 100 salvaged hand and vanity mirrors that hang in the make-up area, and the ribbon of weathered, pressed-tin ceiling tiles that peels downward to define the shop's dramatic entrance.

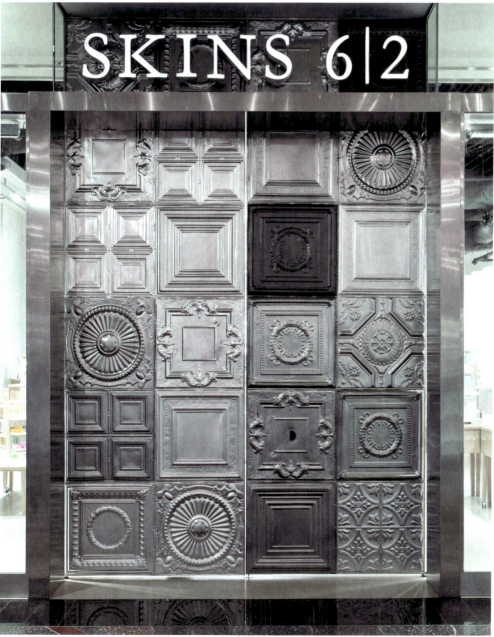

[1]

SYBARITE
Client: Marni

Most of the Marni flagships contrast boldness with simplicity and are dominated by the shop's signature stainless steel display sculptures. In Marni Kobe, the white blankness of the space and large elliptical Barrisol incisions in the ceiling that cast a diffuse light, are offset by a scarlet ceiling that fades into a sanguine ombré as it descends toward the floor. In contrast, the 220-square-meter store at the Crystals in Las Vegas was inspired by the image of a cracking whip suspended as it unfurls in mid-air. Outlining the edges of the space, this sinuous "lasso" of stainless steel provides hang space for the garments. Curving gray walls are interrupted by an array of display bubbles that are randomly concave and convex, backlit and shadowed, creating a textural composition. In the ceiling, giant Barrisol discs echo the bubble motif of the walls and cast soft light, while the polished concrete floor provides a clean backdrop. The 128-square-meter New York shop features an eclectic style matching the area's historical bohemian chic, but is anchored by the unusual branching steel display that is practically a three-dimensional logo for the fashion label.

[2]

[3]

[4]

[5]

Monki Sea of Scallops

2010 / Oslo, Norway

ELECTRIC DREAMS
Client: Monki

For the Swedish clothing label (now under part-ownership of H&M) Stockholm-based Electric Dreams was asked to create an interior in which merchandise could be changed daily and themed for various marketing campaigns throughout the year. The studio separated the retail floor into four zones with a whimsical submarine theme: In one, tidal currents massage the shoe display; jellyfish guard the accessories; bubbles bump the denim shelves; and a submerged merry-go-round rotates the brand's more targeted branding efforts. Throughout the space, wheeled sea horses proffer reconfigurable display surfaces.

248

Moooi Showroom

[1] *2008 / Amsterdam,*
                Netherlands
[2] *2010 / London, UK*

MOOOI
Client: Moooi

The mother of all Moooi showrooms is situated in the artistic heart of Amsterdam, the Jordaan district, the 700-square-meter gallery was renovated in spring 2011 into the ne plus ultra brand experience. Opening the door of any Moooi space is like stepping into an enchanted realm rendered whimsically at different scales and in florid but modern compositions. In the rear, visitors can explore an interactive world of white podia some of which display items from the collection, such as chairs with headsets, around which guests may sit and enjoy fairytales about the "magic world of Moooi." In the center of the gallery, the history of the brand is told in photographs and sketches permanently on display along a dark museum-like corridor. In the Moooi theather nearby, with an installation of Raimond lights, thousands of twinkling stars guarded by a row of noble Horse Lamps by Front. Facing the horses, a multicolored merry-go-round of pieces by Studio Job consists of a clutch of Gothic Chairs arranged in a circle atop a 5 x 5 meter carpet depicting a fantastical seascape.

[1]

[2]

BLESS Home
2011 / Berlin, Germany

BLESS
Client: BLESS Shop

Open to the public for only four hours a week and otherwise by appointment only, the Bless concept shop, designed by Cyril Duval of Item Idem together with the Bless fashion designers, is situated on a typical residential street in East Berlin. As its location would suggest, it is, indeed, styled as the apartment of the archetypal and original BLESS collector, a fictional and extremely fortunate personage who lives surrounded by BLESS products in a flat that will change and grow over time, as any home is wont to. A climb to the third-floor walkup is rewarded with a visit to this intimate, personalized space where voyeurs and Bless fans, alike, may remain as long as they like as long as they've made an appointment. Clients are allowed to explore as they wish: sip a tea, pull a book from the shelf to read on the balcony, poke through the cupboards or daydream while wrapped up in the hammock. In future, BLESS Home may even become a bed and breakfast.

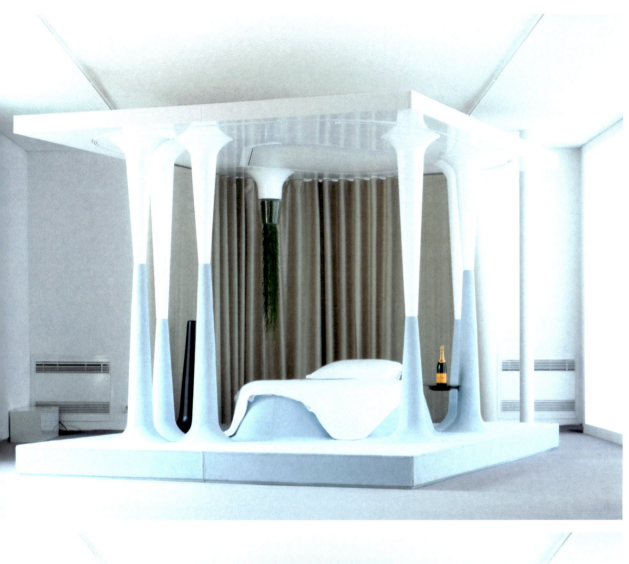

Once Upon a Dream
2010 / Reims, France

MATHIEU LEHANNEUR
Client: Veuve Clicquot Ponsardin

Apparently, the widowed Madame Clicquot, founder of legendary champagne label Veuve Clicquot Ponsardin, suffered from insomnia. How fitting then that French designer Lehanneur created an automated bedroom and an ideal sanctuary in which to recuperate from jetlag or mere workaday sleeplessness in the company's Hôtel de Marc retreat in Reims. The designer used data gathered in physiological studies for treating people who suffer from chronic insomnia to create a room with black-out curtains and chromatherapy that, second to a few glasses of bubbly, may be the best way to ensure sweet dreams.

Francfranc

2010 / Nagoya, Japan

GLAMOROUS:
YASUMICHI MORITA
Client: BALS Corporation
See also page 196

The first FrancFranc concept shop and "museum outlet" outside Tokyo is located in Nagoya City and was conceived in terms of a "shop as museum." The tagline "Lifestyle with Art" informs the interior scheme, imagining a life lived both artfully and close to art. The outlet has three floors and many surprises, including a mammoth chandelier at the entrance that looks different when seen from here than it does as one ascends the double stair behind it. On the second floor, the large scale of a long, two-story-high display dwarfs visitors in an awing way while furniture, CDs, and magazines are available beside a cafe on the third floor. Photo frames painted by the artist Masataka Kurashina dot the facade, changing their contents between daytime and night.

Camper Shop
2009 / Tokyo, Japan

JAIME HAYON -
HAYON STUDIO BCN
Client: Camper
See also page 260

Inspired by classical circus elements, Hayon's Tokyo Camper footwear shop is filled with enchanting, colorful details. Shaped like a candy cane, the front door handle announces immediately that surprises await visitors within. Hayon mostly eschewed hard edges, preferring radiused corners, curved biomorphic shapes, and tapering legs. Walls covered in Bisazza mosaic tiles stand in contrast to the unfinished cement floor while bevelled glass panels reminiscent of cut gemstones partition the space and tinted mirrors mounted to the ceiling elongate perspective and lend the shop warmth.

ALV
2009 / Milan, Italy

FABIO NOVEMBRE, PATRIZIO MOZZICAFREDDO, LORENZO DE NICOL
Client: Alviero Martini

Fashion designer Alviero Martini's 465-square-meter Milan shop takes its cues from the natural and particularly human compulsion to keep moving. The designers represented the eternal and unchanging movements of the planets in a huge dilating white atom that happens to serve as handbag display as well. They describe the space as a fluid interchange of centrifugal surfaces and centripetal reflexes, in other words, a tenuous balance between freedom and dependence.

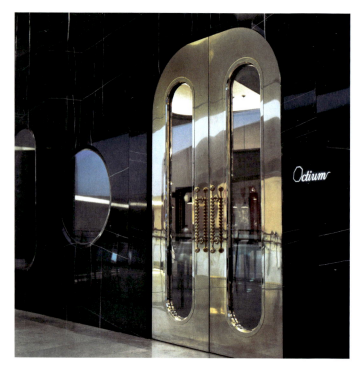

Octium Jewelry
2009 / Kuwait City, Kuwait

JAIME HAYON -
HAYON STUDIO BCN
Client: Octium Jewelry
See also page 256

This concept jewelry shop adorns a mall in Kuwait, which presents the work of designers from around the globe. Hayon applied his signature tapering, through-the-looking-glass aesthetic and bespoke pieces in contrasting finishes, including glossy lacquered woods, natural oak, ceramic, and lush fabrics.

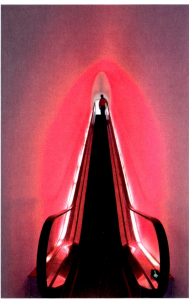

Barbie Shanghai
2008 / Shanghai, China

SLADE ARCHITECTURE
Client: Mattel

The first 10,000-square-meter Barbie flagship store grew up in Shanghai not New York, unlike the doll herself. For toy giant Mattel, Manhattan architects at Slade designed a store where "Barbie is hero," introducing Barbie as a global lifestyle brand by emphasizing the doll's historical link to fashion. The store's façade combines references to fashion, product packaging, decorative arts, and architectural iconography and consists of two layers: molded, translucent polycarbonate interior panels and flat exterior glass panels printed with a feminine lattice frit pattern. The lobby features curvaceous, pearlescent surfaces and leads to a pink escalator tube while, at the store's core, 800 Barbie dolls corset the three-story spiral staircase. The design results in a youthful space where optimism and possibility become expressions of a woman's best assets.

Lunar
Pop-Up Store
2011 / Shanghai, China

///BYN: NICOLAS SALTO DEL GIORGIO, BITTOR SANCHEZ-MONASTERIO, GUO ZHICHUAN, LI MIN

Client: Private European Art Foundation

Lunar popped up for one month in Shanghai to host an exhibition and store for a private European art institution, but was also built to travel and conform to divergent spaces. Inhabiting the interior of a warehouse-like space, this highly graphical 250-square-meter, 114-cubic-meter metal-frame assemblage is the result of an aggregation of 20 geometric forms. Local architects ///byn fabricated each six-cubic-meter module in one of two standard shapes with a shiny black exterior and soft yellow interior to introduce a different product useful for daily living on the lunar surface. ///byn organized the modular architecture to mimic the limited space of a moon capsule. The lack of any Cartesian reference forced visitors to move through the interiors via a restricted route, triggering behavior amongst visitors that might be more usual in a zero-gravity environment.

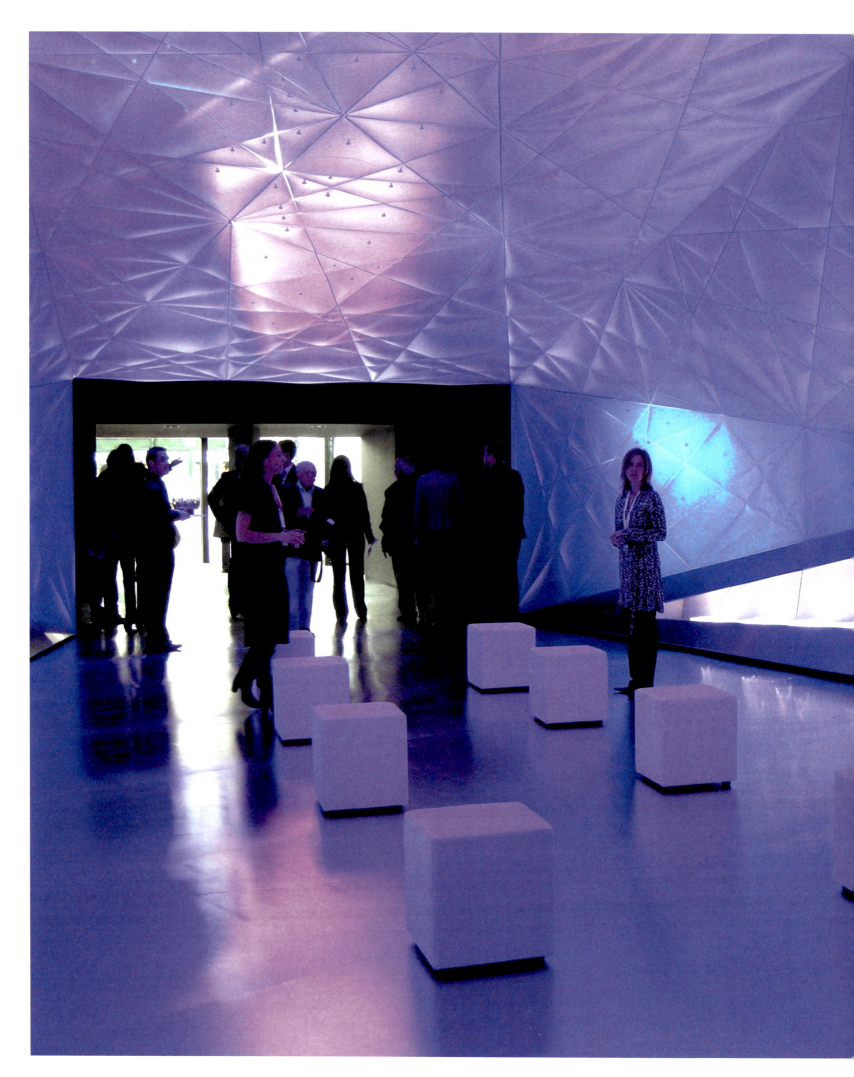

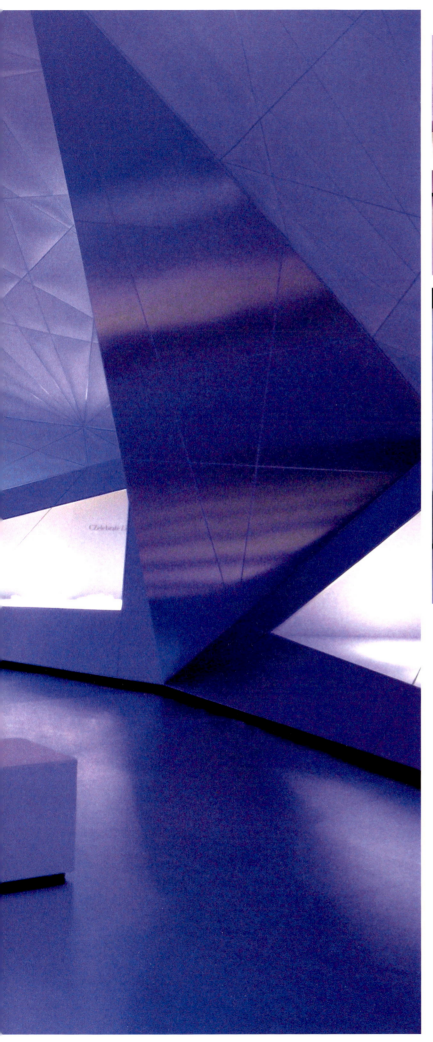

Ambient Gem

*2008 / Basel,
Switzerland*

VEECH MEDIA ARCHITECTURE

Client: D. Swarovski & Co., Enlightened
Swarovski TM

During the week-long Baselworld
Watch & Jewellery Show, Vienna studio
VMA's 400-square-meter trade fair
stand for the Enlightened Swarovski
Elements gemstone brand was based
on translating our fascination with
precious stones into a sensual three-
dimensional experience. The form of
the space followed the logic of a folded
crystalline structure, and conceals the
extremely limiting and banal geometry
of the existing outer tent. The structure
was composed of a pneumatic membrane divided into inflated facets and
featured complex alternating lighting
and sound design that created a subtle
visual, acoustic, and tactile experience.
Animated graphics by celebrated British graphic designer Neville Brody/Re-
search Studios also depicted Swarovski's new brand.

State Grid Pavilion — Magic Box

2010 / Shanghai, China

ATELIER BRÜCKNER

Client: IBM China for State Grid
Corporation of China

Designed by Stuttgart's Atelier
Brückner for the Chinese government's
electrical utility, the Magic Box became
the pulsating heart of the State Grid
Pavilion at EXPO Shanghai for several
months. Electrical impulses were
emitted from the Box to flow over the
skin of the building complex through
power-charged grid lines. This tight
grid of LEDs also threaded the inner
walls of the 15-meter-high cube,
essentially building a room through
light effects that caged visitors on six
sides. Through dramatic images, a film
conveyed the company's mission: the
reliable supply of energy to the national
grid, leading to improvements in urban
quality of life. Visitors were immersed
in a spatial installation that generated
an emotionally charged experience
powered by hope for the future.

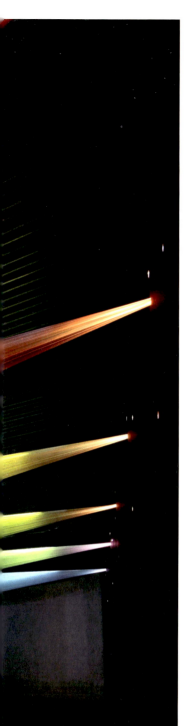

Neoreal Wonder
2011 / Milan, Italy

WOW
Client: Canon

Marking the fourth year of Canon's immersive Neoreal installations during the one-week Milan Furniture Fair, Tokyo-based Torafu and Florence-based WOW designed a "light loom," consisting of hundreds of 0.5 mm-thick strands of leveling cord, each strung at a length of 16 meters. The loom served as a physical manifestation of projected light, a functional sculp-ture spelling the word "wonder" along one wall and, massed in this way, a projection screen. The strands carried imagery (made by WOW with Canon equipment and displayed by 20 Canon projectors) entitled Circle of Light, that compressed longer-term events into a few moments, like a time-lapse film. Each letter was anchored to a single point on one side of the gallery, while its constituent strings reached outward and downward to just above visitors' heads. A berm-like element in the floor encouraged people to recline and relax while watching the film on large curved screens that flanked either side of the room.

DJS The Beauty of Facets

2008 / Hong Kong, China

PANORAMA:
HORACE PAN,
ALAN TSE,
VIVIAN CHAN
Client: Chinese Arts & Crafts (HK) Ltd.

The interior concept for The Beauty of Facets, a jewellery label selling diamond and jade, is a total branding exercise that targets a middle-class demographic. The concept seems simple: the design takes its cues from the chemical structures and cut facets of gemstones and begins with a white envelope of alabaster wall displays and white marble flooring, which provide a clear, minimal frame for the space. Then Hong Kong-based Panorama installed luminous wall-mounted vitrines with randomly tilted vertical faces in celadon-hues that echo the color and translucency of jade. Rows of floating glazed shadowboxes in various sizes and heights generate a rhythm and texture that adds complexity and animation to the room. Add to these surfaces their reflections in the slanted mirror polished stainless steel ceiling panels and you get a distortion that amplifies the sculptural quality of the space and—much as the jewels do—leaves clients happily bedazzled.

C_42:
Citroën Flagship
Showroom
2002 / Paris, France

MANUELLE GAUTRAND

Client: Automobiles Citroën

The 1200-square-meter Citroën showroom remakes the automaker's original 1920s home at No. 42 Champs Elysées in Paris. Gautrand added chevrons, lozenges, and triangles to the minimalist glass facade and, as the building ascends, nearly three-dimensional prisms. At the top, it becomes a grand sculpture that resembles origami. The shape of the building was inspired by the abstracted shape of a car while the brand's signature red adorns glass panels but is masked slightly by a filter built into the finished glass. This also minimizes the heat of the sun and creates a diaphanous, pearly white atmosphere inside. The architect sought to create a museum-like space, but more beautiful than the "artifacts" on show inside is the view of the Paris sky from the roof, accessed via a panoramic lift; one of the most awesome vehicles in the building.

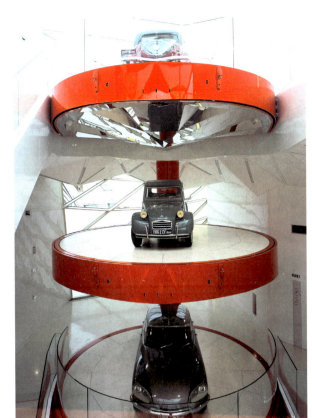

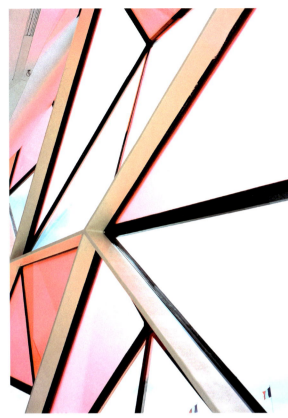

Voestalpine Stahlwelt
2009 / Linz, Austria

KMS TEAM
Client: Voestalpine AG

This Austrian steel company commissioned German designers KMS to design a brand museum and visitor center with five levels of interactive exhibits leading visitors from the steel production process through the experience of the finished product. The center includes accessible spheres set up as terminals, interactive handrails, and a vertical conveyor belt that demystifies the making of steel. The steel experience is showcased in a giant "pot," flooded with pulsating light and surrounded by a 700-square-foot LED envelope. Inside, 80 chrome steel spheres with a diameter of up to 2.5 meters represent the abstracted atoms that float on the molten steel balls, arranged according to the molecular structure of iron. The installation won a Silver Award for Environmental Design at the 2010 CLIO Awards.

Index

Tobias Rehberger
Germany / www.tobiasrehberger.de
Pages 28 - 31
Nothing Happens for a Reason
at Logomo Café © Tobias Rehberger /
Furniture: Artek and Tobias Rehberger /
Photography: Bo Stranden

Tokujin Yoshioka
Japan / www.tokujin.com
Page 126
The Invisibles by Tokujin Yoshioka

Tomás Alonso
UK / www.tomas-alonso.com
Pages 24 - 25
Camper Shop London, Glasgow, Genoa
Photography: Sánchez & Montoro

Torafu Architects
Japan / www.torafu.com
Pages 130 - 131
NIKE 1LOVE
Construction + Manufacturing: Ishimaru,
Mihoya Glass / Photography: Daici Ano

U

UdK Bookshop: Dalia Butvidaite, Leonard Steidle, Johannes Drechsler
Germany / www.udk-buchshop.de
Page 78
UdK Bookshop
Organisation: Florian Hennig, Eric Zapel
/ Professor: Florian Riegler /
Assistants: Dipl.Ing. Jeanne-Françoise
Fischer, AA Dipl. Karoline Markus /
Graphics: Jonas Lindström /
Photography: Reiner Hausleiter

UNA Arquitetos
Brazil / www.unaarquitetos.com.br
Pages 208 - 209
Garoa Store
Photography: Leonardo Finotti

United Nude
USA / www.unitednude.com
Pages 152 - 153
United Nude Flagship Store New York 1
Photography: United Nude

Urban A&O
USA / www.urbanao.com
Pages 120 - 121
Mortal Coil Photography:Tom Hennes

UXUS
Netherlands / www.uxus.com
Pages 60 - 61
Dutch Masters, Schiphol Museum Shop
Photography: Dim Balsem
Pages 230 - 233
H&M Home Home Reflections Showroom
Photography: Dim Balsem
Page 241
Skins 6/2 Cosmetics

V

Veech Media Architecture
Austria / www.veech-vma.com
Pages 266 - 267
Ambient Gem
Photography: Eveline Tietze-Tilley

W

WE Architecture
Denmark / www.we-a.dk
Pages 134 -135
T Magi Photography: Enok Holsegård

We Made This
UK / www.wemadethis.co.uk
Pages 68 - 69
Hoxton Street Monster Supplies

Wilson Brothers
UK / www.wilsonbrothers.co.uk
Pages 64 - 65
Raise your game
Photography: Roger Harris,
Oscar Wilson (upper right small)
Pages 182 - 183
Rapha Mobile Cycle Club
Photography: Jens Marrot (upper left,
upper right), Oscar Wilson

Wonderwall Inc.
Japan / www.wonder-wall.com
Pages 22 - 23
Pass the Baton Omotesdando
Photography: Kozo Takayama
Pages 128 - 129
Nike Harajuku

WOW
Japan / **www.w0w.co.jp**
Pages 272 - 273
Neoreal Wonder

Y

Yasutaka Yoshimura Architects Inc.
Japan / www.ysmr.com
Page 80
Paperbag Igloo
Photography: Yasutaka Yoshimura

Z

Z-A: Guy Zucker
USA / www.z-astudio.com
Page 84
Delicatessen Clothing Store
Photography: Naomi Yogev,
Shay Ben Efraim
Pages 116 - 117
Delicatessen Clothing Store
Team: Dan Affleck, Adam Hostetler,
Leo Mulvehill, Guy Zucker / Photography:
Assaf Pinchuk

ZMIK designers
Switzerland / www.zmik.ch
Page 32 - 33
Artshop 09
Photography: Eik Frenzel & ZMIK
Page 81
Artshop 10
Photography: Eik Frenzel & ZMIK

Out of the Box!

Brand Experiences between Pop-Up and Flagship

Edited by Robert Klanten, Sven Ehmann, and Kitty Bolhöfer
Text and preface by Shonquis Moreno

Cover and layout by Kasper Zwaaneveld for Gestalten
Cover photography by Bo Stranden, *Nothing Happens for a Reason* by Tobias Rehberger
Typefaces: Malaussène by Laure Afchain, Planeta by Dani Klauser
Foundry: www.gestaltenfonts.com

Project management by Julian Sorge for Gestalten
Project management assistance by Minh Bui for Gestalten
Production management by Janine Milstrey for Gestalten
Proofreading by Bettina Klein
Printed by Offsetdruckerei Karl Grammlich GmbH
Made in Germany

Published by Gestalten, Berlin 2011
ISBN 978-3-89955-374-1

For more information, please visit www.gestalten.com.

Bibliographic information published by the Deutsche Nationalbibliothek.
The Deutsche Nationalbibliothek lists this publication in the Deutsche
Nationalbibliografie; detailed bibliographic data are available online at
http://dnb.d-nb.de.

None of the content in this book was published in exchange for payment by
commercial parties or designers; Gestalten selected all included work based solely
on its artistic merit.

This book was printed according to the internationally accepted ISO 14001
standards for environmental protection, which specify requirements for an
environmental management system.

This book was printed on paper certified by the FSC®.

MIX
Paper from
responsible sources
FSC® C011712

Gestalten is a climate-neutral company. We collaborate with the non-profit carbon
offset provider myclimate (www.myclimate.org) to neutralize the company's
carbon footprint produced through our worldwide business activities by investing
in projects that reduce CO_2 emissions (www.gestalten.com/myclimate).

412361